FLIX

Clips from a Filmmaker's Odyssey

Mick Benderoth

Dedication

For my wife

Nancy

who turned a man-child into

a man

Acknowledgments

Many thanks to my astounding editor Woody Gimbel, my good friend, alpha reader Art Lasky, and Thad Rutkowski, whose writer's workshops, "Telling Great Stories", started me on the path to writing prose. A special thank you to Krystine Kercher for working with me on formatting and layout of the interior of the book as well as for the cover, and for her assistance in publishing this book.

Mick Benderoth, 2023, NYC

Epigraph

"Sometimes reality is too complex.
Stories give it form."
Jean-Luc Godard

Contents

She Was...i

Maternal 1

Gift 5

Icebox...13

Thumb..17

Home Run 23

Icehouse 29

Callinectes sapidus...35

Gone Fishing..39

Jazz...45

Gem..53

Jimi Hendrix 63

Progeny 69

Living War Dead 77

Promise 83

Shilly 89

European Customs..101

Hunt 113

Jimi Jam...121

Songbird...127

Spider Guy..135

Dream Job 145

Hubris 153

Chutzpah 161

Taormina 173

Kick The Cane 179

String Bean 185

Popie 193

Brotherhood 199

What's in a Name? 207

Writing on the Wall 211

Advice 217

Bliss 225

Tres J's 231

Sunshine 241

Epilogue 247

About The Author 251

She Was

A poem for my beloved wife Nancy

She was
She was
She was

A girl by chance I knew
who walked so sure not slow
A woman on her way
Far places she did go

So fast I could not see
a side I did not know
a secret kept so well
one she dares not show

a muse to men she drew
and women they could be
so like her as she flew
passed them sure and free

she was
she was
she was

not being what she saw
bringing things so new
changing all the rules
a wild wind when it blew

a strong defiant view
timeless out of time
she loved me if I grew
so I could make her mine

she took me far away
then brought me home again
to witness a new way
to put the thought to pen

she was
she was
she was

travails along her path
not hold her back for long
made her stronger still
so I could write and sing her song

she danced above the fray,
to catch her was to win the prize
one that lasts not long
for even perfect life must die

she fought so hard so long
yet never showed her pain
she called my name out loud
so to her side I came

to watch her light grow faint,
then flicker, and was gone
eternal like the stars,
a glitter that goes on and on

alone I face a life
to build it day by day
her spirit guides me on
the pain will go away

she was
she was
she was

memories she left
seem like she is near
flashes of her past
still are fresh and clear

there may never be
one so filled with life
will I ever see again
someone to fill her space

alone I face a life
to build it day by day
her spirit guides me on
the pain will go away

she was
she was
she was

memory will not die
then becomes a myth
like a breathless sigh
with a final kiss

she is
she is
she is

Maternal

Swaddled in a nursery crib at tiny Mercy Hospital, Baltimore, Maryland, May 8, 1945, I was born…on V.E. Day. Stopped the war in diapers. I am saved from my tongue tangling moniker, Alexander Eddison Benderoth Jr. by my Irish grandfather, John Joseph McKenna, who leaned over my crib, his leprechaun grin beaming, voice echoing his roughish brogue, *"Aye, there's a Mick if I er' I seen one."* *Mick* being old slang for an Irishman. I became "The Mick", then Mickey, now just Mick.

My mother, Mary Teresa McKenna Benderoth, five foot two, eyes of blue, ninety pounds if rain drenched, easy on the eye, as they usta say. Hailed as the spunky, ambitious lass of the McKenna clan. Mary married a sailor, Ben Benderoth, now shipboard somewhere in the Atlantic. Mom and I were the only residents in the maternity ward, my birth by caesarian. My mother, stomach stitched, in her private room. Me in the vacant nursery. She refused pain meds. They didn't agree with her.

Sweltering, humid, southern night air oozes through the open window behind my crib. Baltimore was alive with the VE Day celebration. A city wide carnivalesque shout out, climax…a dazzling fireworks display.

Mary smells smoke, not acrid sulfurous firework smoke but *fire* smoke filling her room. She sees it looming in the hall. Maternal instinct slams into high gear. Her baby at risk.

Painfully, crawls out of bed, risks ripping the sutures stitching her incision. Finds the nurse station unattended. She calls out. Nothing. Yells out. Nothing. Everyone's outside watching fireworks. Edges her way to the nursery. Sees the source of choking smoke, pouring in the window behind my crib. The building beside the hospital aflame, my window curtains scorched, ash flakes float to my blanket. Her sutured incision throbbing, Mary winces, her pain masked by *mother love* as she scoops me from the crib, scuttles to her room. She opens the window and clears the smoke, her room being on the opposite side of the burning building. She plops me bed center, secured by pillows, closes the door, and shuffles back to the nurse's station where she grabs a desk phone. She dials zero and gets the operator, "I'm a patient at Mercy Hospital. The building next door is on fire. I'm alone with my infant son. Please alert the fire department."

The operator complies. Mom uses the station's rolling desk chair for support back to her room. Our room. She nuzzles as she slides in bed beside me. Sirens blare as the fire trucks arrive. The blaze is soon extinguished.

Mary's bravery makes the Baltimore Sun. A photo with me in her arms. This extraordinary woman gave me life, saved my life. Mary Theresa McKenna Benderoth. My hero. My mother.

Gift

"*It's alive!!! it's alive!!*" Victor Frankenstein's crazed rant as he leans over the sheet-covered creature he had made from severed arms, legs, head, brain, of various corpses stolen by his crippled grave robber, Igor. My younger brother Steve and I sat in awe, our eyes riveted to the black and white images on the movie screen.

We were movie freaks since we were old enough to walk to the greatest place on earth, The Waverly Movie Theater in Baltimore. The theater was a rundown, chipped, weather-stained brick building. A landmark, its marque blazing the venue in giant red letters, *Frankenstein, The Wolfman! Dracula! War of the Worlds!* Classic horror and sci-fi flicks.

Every Saturday our folks gave each of us a quarter to pay the eighteen-cents admission, with enough left over for a box of candy. Steve, Goober's *Raisinets*. Me, a box of *Good and Plenty*.

Every Saturday we walked to Waverly to catch the latest double feature plus a serial. Always a cliffhanger that left the heroine near death to be rescued by the hero in next week's episode. When we viewed the Universal Classic, *The Wolfman*, Steve was so terrified when the cursed man, Larry Talbot transformed into a monstrous, snarling werewolf, he bolted from his seat, dashed up the aisle to hide in the back of the theater. I did notice that he kept turning his head back to catch the action. A love-hate moment for sure.

We left the Waverly imagining the movies we would make someday. Not why they were made, but how. A man turns into a werewolf, an Indian's arrow thrust into a cowboy's bleeding chest, a switch blade knife thrown sticking into a gangster's back, *The Rocket Man*, soaring through the clouds, King Kong the infamous, humongous ape, swinging from The Empire State Building, Fay Ray grasped in the giant ape's hand screaming for dear life as bi-wing airplanes machine gunned Kong to death.

All fodder for the masterpieces we would create not *if*, no *ifs* about it, but...*WHEN! we got to Hollywood. Land of silver screen dreams.*

Christmas Eve, 1954 "The night before Christmas." I was ten, Steve eight. So overexcited as we place a plate of home baked sugar cookies, plus a tall glass of milk on the coffee table, for...*you know who.* We were still sort of believers and wanted to be and could hardly get to sleep, then woke up way too early. My parents wisely started a ritual of putting our budging Christmas Stockings on our foot bed posts to allow them a few hours of sleep. We dive in. Wrapping paper confetti airborne.

Stockings ransacked, we'd pounce onto our mom and dad's double bed, chanting, *"Can we go down now? Please! Please! Please!"* Bleary eyed, they robed and slippered, leading us down the pine garland wrapped stairway banister, into our living room. The piney smell of evergreen fills the air.

"Look, Steve," I point. Gone were the cookies! Milk glass empty! Santa had been here!

We drift into a Christmas Wonderland that appeared overnight. A massive floor to ceiling Scotch pine tree, decorated to the ninety nines. fancy-wrapped presents, large, small, oblong, and round, piled high beneath, spilling onto the living room rug. Hardly a space to walk. We'd been good boys. Santa was good back.

Steve's first present, *Elvis Presley's* first single "That's all *right.*" Mine, Bill Haley and the Comets "Rock around the

Clock." Rock and roll classics that would soon reveal a musical path we would later follow playing in myriads of rock bands on our way to Hollywood. Movies first. Music follows.

All presents opened, our dad brought in a huge box wrapped in silver foil. What could it be...something so humongous? We dove into it to find a tiny box wrapped in the same paper. In the box, a note "Search for the next box." Steve and I looked everywhere, with Mom and Dad hinting, "Cold, colder, warm, warmer, hot... hotter... ON FIRE!"

We stood in front of the kitchen cabinet usually filled with canned goods. Inside was another silver-wrapped, medium-sized box. We began peeling off the paper. We screamed in unison when we saw the word "Kodak." Hearts pounding, we ripped off the rest of the paper. Holy mackerel!!! Our greatest gift, a *Kodak Brownie 8mm Home Movie Camera*. It was a simple box with a lens and a spring motor...but it made movies. We were on our way.

Instead of the usual home movies of family gatherings, vacations, and parties, Steve and I made real movies, monster flicks, action flicks, comedy larks. We invited friends and family to view the latest M&S (Mick and Steve) Production.

Years passed, movie camera technology advanced, and we took the next step into 16m, the format for TV news and documentaries. Ever self-encouraged, "M & S" brainstormed our next epic. Then...Dead stop! Graver concerns. Harsh reality, turning eighteen, getting unwanted birthday gifts. Notices to sign up with the governments *Selective Service* to be eligible for the draft into the army. Shivers down my spine, as I imagined the consequences.

Fortunately, instead of being listed *"1-A," sound and fit for duty*, we got 2S deferments, both headed for college. Knowing after graduation we would again be the dreaded, 1-A. Unfazed, we actively protested the war. The spark for our next M&S Production came from TV News, announcing "The March on The Pentagon," October 21, 1967. The first ever national demonstration protesting an American War. Our next film, a no brainer, a documentary, "The March! Against the war in Vietnam."

We drove the six plus hours from Baltimore to Washington, bumper to bumper traffic. Busses, cars jam-packed, headed to the protest. Parking a half mile away. Donned with fake *Press Passes*, dressed in suits and ties, unlike the hippie dress of most protestors, we began the trek. Protesters, with anti-war signs and banners appeared everywhere, marching to the objective: the nerve center of the American Military, The Pentagon.

We were caught in the throng. I held out the camera and forged ahead, coming face-to face with cold reality, a phalanx of armed soldiers, forming a seemingly impenetrable wall, several hundred feet from our objective. We flashed our fake passes, the troops, stone-faced, did not budge, "We're the Press!," we screamed. They did not flinch. The protest stopped dead-for a moment, but the frenzied crowd was relentless. A human wave plowed through the troops, knocking many to the ground. The troops were overwhelmed, powerless, trampled. The marchers pressed on. No stopping now.

Filming everything in sight, passing the camera back and forth, Steve and I were propelled onward, then there it was...The Pentagon, surrounded by even more troops. This did not slow the protestors. Engulfed by wave upon wave of bodies, we were literally carried by the crowd, camera running. Nothing could stop the onslaught, until something did. A small, metal can rolled into the masses, then exploded! Tear gas! Our eyes burned, our throats, raked with acrid air. We could not breathe. *The first time America's youth were tear gassed by America's youth.* Young US soldiers against American civilian protestors. One wearing military uniforms, the other, jeans and flowered shirts. The most vehement protestors braved the gas, we were right with them.

Filming The Pentagon through the choking haze of gas was horrifying and exciting, and we achieved what we came for, we got *"The Shot,"* *a long hair bearded youth bursting through the line of armed soldiers waving a charred American flag,* used in our short Maryland Film Festival, Silver in Atlanta and Philadelphia Festivals. *Abraxas* was soon followed by another festival winner, our anti-war drama, *A Beautiful Day For A Picnic.*

We beat the draft. Me, getting a deferment teaching science at Baltimore suburban High School, Steve, a letter from a left-wing family doctor who prescribed Steve had flat feet.

Steve left Baltimore for NYC, starting his quest for his musical bliss. I soon followed beginning my journey to Hollywood. All because of the greatest gift, our Kodak Brownie 8mm Home Movie Camera. Still sitting scratched, dented, fifty years later, on my office bookcase.

My youthful odyssey began.

Icebox

Memory. Icebox. I'm six. Nineteen fifty-one. Icebox. Ubiquitous, rectangular, white slab against the kitchen wall. Two doors. Top. Bottom. I love ice day. The iceman cometh. A massive block of ice between rusty tongs rests on his shoulder. Grandma opens the top door. The iceman slides the block in. Cold food for a week. I follow him out to the alley, his truck stacked with ice. He icepicks me off a chunk, smiles, I smile back. Yum.

Later that summer, a big day. Our first refrigerator. The movers put the icebox on the back porch for the junk man. We all stand in awe in front of this big, white machine. Dad plugs it in. When it gets cold, food goes in. No more iceman. No more ice blocks. No more ice chips to slurp. Now, ice cubes. It makes me sad.

Out on the porch playing, I stop, stand at the ancient icebox, waiting to be picked up by the junkman. Get a bad idea. I open the bottom door, just big enough. I slide in, close it. *Thunk!* It's dark. Too dark. Quiet. Too quiet. Had enough. I want out. Feel around for handle. There is none. Outside only. I panic. Scream! Scream! Scream! Nobody. Isolated, me, totally isolated. My knees cramp up. Painful. Keep screaming, nothing. Hard to breathe. Gasp. Choke. Dizzy. Sleepy. *Am I dying? Am I?* Then . . . nothing. *Out cold in the ice box.*

I wake up. *Where?* Groggy, monster headache. A big black rubber thing covers my nose and mouth. I hear the words "He's going to be all right." Turn my head. It's a doctor in

Baltimore General Hospital's ER. I sit up. My mom, tears streaming, hugs tight. I cry too. Hug her tight back. The doctor says, "They tell you to rip out the gaskets. Nobody listens. Five kids died last week. You're a lucky boy."

When we get home, the icebox is gone. Dinner time. The new white refrigerator dominates the kitchen. They call it icebox. I shiver, quiver. I call it the fridge.

Thumb

Checkers. My favorite game. I got a set for my seventh birthday, and my younger brother Steve was five, he and I were having a tournament, winner three out of five, who get the crown. It was time for our daily match, but Steve was nowhere to be found. Very strange, we were sidekicks.

I went upstairs to our bedroom, looked in, no Steve. I started out, heard soft whimpering from under the bed. I knelt down, there he was, tears streaming down his flushed cheeks, thumb in his mouth "What are you doing under there?" "I questioned. "Hiding...Mom wants to put more of that stuff on my thumb, to stop me from sucking. It tastes terrible, gives me a belly ache," he sobbed.

Steve had been sucking his thumb from day one. He even learned to speak intelligibly with his thumb parked in his mouth. He did take it out when he ate but had to sit on his hand to keep his thumb at bay. It seemed to have a mind of its own, his second-best friend, me being first, I hoped.

The year he started kindergarten last year, he came home crying, adamantly refusing to go back. "They pointed and laughed at me," he cried. Mom talked to the head of the kindergarten. Steve was allowed to suck his thumb at recess, but not in class. It was useless, still he tried, and tried and tried. A whole year of torture with no change.

Summer passed. Steve was going into first grade. This was the big time, real school. He was terrified. Sucked faster when he got nervous.

All dressed up for the big day, Steve and I walked to school together. Me, in second grade, Steve in first. He came to a dead stop at the school steps. "I can't go in" he blubbered.

"You have to, the truant officer will come out and get you," something my mom told me to say if this happened, which it did.

"I don't care, I can't do it."

I took his hand, "I'll walk you to your classroom, you'll be ok," I promised.

He gave me his wary look and spoke nary a word, just squeezed my hand harder, as I tugged him up the steps, through the big glass doors, down the hall. His sucking got faster, and faster as we got to his room.

The teacher came out smiling, "You must be Steve, we've been waiting for you so we could pledge the flag."

His hand glued to mine, he sucked at top speed. The teacher took his other hand, I shook him loose. Steve's eyes started tearing up. The teacher took him into the classroom starting to close the door. He was looking forlornly over his shoulder at me, his eyes screaming, Help me! Help me! I felt so horrible, I almost cried myself.

I went to my classroom. All I could think about was Steve. The anguish, the torture, the humiliation.

Three o'clock, the bell rang. Thank the thumb god, school's over. I raced to Steve's room to pick him up. Steve was the last one out. Me, dumbfounded. His thumb was not in this mouth, right hand at his side.

I asked, "Are you ok? "Un huh," he murmured. "What happened? You're not..."

He cut me off. "There was this other boy in class, sucked his thumb too. They called him "Sucky," like that was his name. Sucky!, Sucky!, Sucky!, The teacher didn't say anything. I didn't want them to call me sucky or any other name, my name is Steve, so...I just stopped."

"Just like that?" He nodded proudly.

20

I knew school was for learning. Some things not in books or on the blackboard.

Steve learned something big that day. Never sucked again.

Home Run

Sports...take 'em or leave 'em...me, leave 'em, any kind, playing or watching. Third grade. Dodgeball. I never could see it coming. Thump, I was out again. Softball, it's bigger than a baseball. Never hit it, ever.

My fourth-grade teacher, Mr. Kastner, a gifted, sensitive teacher, found part of my problem. A school idol for his gift of understanding what it was like to be a kid, and treating us as equals, he was concerned that I was always asking to move closer and closer to the front of the room.

"Mick what's going on?," Mr. K. asked caringly.

I was embarrassed to say, but had to, "I can't see the blackboard...unless I'm up close."

"Have you parents ever had your vision tested?"

"No, sir."

"May I ask why?"

"My father thinks glasses are a crutch, a weakness. He's doesn't like his kids to be weak."

Mr. Kastner was gentle with his astonishment. Unknown to me, called home, talked with my mother. She explains her dilemma. He sternly tells her that if she could not get me tested for glasses, then he would. Shamed, my mother, defied my father...got me glasses. He says nothing. Powerless, fearful of official authority, a reoccurring sign of his innate cowardice, typical of his bullying persona

I could see. It was a miracle, still could compensate for years of poor vision. Still could not hit a ball. My younger brother, Steve could. My father intimated that he was glad at least one of his sons was athletic. He bought Steve a baseball glove. The two of them played catch for hours, while I looked on shamefully.

Such is life. I got used to being the last one chosen. Swallowed feelings of inadequacy. I moved on to other more gratifying pursuits. My perceptive grandfather helped me along. He bought me a chemistry set. Helped me with the experiments. I learned to love science. Still, inside, I longed to prove myself athletically...someday.

I thought that day had come, when I was 17 on a picnic with a bunch of schoolmates, including my girlfriend, Susie Lane, a cheerleader. Steve and Jeff Bix, the star quarterback on our championship school team part of the gang.

Jeff called for a game of touch. Everybody was up for it, except me. My stomach squinched at the thought. Again, last chosen, Jeff smirked placing me way back, far, far from the line of scrimmage where I could do the least damage.

By the fourth game, everyone was exhausted, save Jeff, who never wore out and me who never ran much anyway. Then "Hut...2....3. I took off down the field, turned, as the football magically landed right in my arms, cradled like a baby. My latent instinct kicked in. I ran like a slow wind. Leaving both teams behind, heading for the goal line. I could hear my teammates screaming and yelling. No one was anywhere near me. My moment of victory at hand, as I crossed the goal line.

My teammates ran towards me still cheering, until I heard not cheers...but jeers...and laughter. I had run the wrong way. No wonder it was so easy. Crushed again, forever dubbed "Wrong Way Benderoth," the word "Sports" deleted from my vocabulary.

Ten years later. I now live in Manhattan, I do not know the name of any New York sports team, or what the hell the Super Bowl was, could care less.

Then it happens again. I am a sought-after film editor cutting a promising feature film, surrounded by top assistants, culled over years, all fast friends.

One morning, twelve other editors and their staffs relax at the coffee machine during break time with my brother Steve, a jingle writer, coincidently scored a commercial with another editor. We're chatting catch up.

Ray Banning, the owner of the editing complex I rent from, bursts in the reception area with his usual over exuberance, "It's that time again, kids!" Ears picked up. Ray, "Our annual softball game, gear and beer on me. I'll choose my teams. Mick, being our senior member will choose his. August 15th game time. Ray's out the door. I'm speechless.

My old nemesis attacks, stomach gripped with nausea...sports. Simple solution. I back out. Not so easy. Besieged by my assistants, my brother, other editors and their staff all wanting to be on my team. Ray is not a crowd favorite. Realizing this, he reenters with a used Maxwell House coffee can. "This will make it easy. Blue marbles Mick, red, me." He shakes. They pick. Teams set. Me comatose. My brother, athletic star of my family, rabid competitor, now Ray's pitcher.

The game is one week away. The potential horror never leaves my mind as I rush to finish this film.

D-Day. Everybody at the field but me, feigning that I have to deliver my project ASAP, hoping the game will end before I show.

I finish early. My stature as a straight shooter on the line, I slink to the elevator, take a cab to the field.

As soon as I show, my assistant Jim rushes me, "Mick, thank god. Bottom of the ninth. They lead three to two. Our last player got to second. You're up."

Should I heave right here, sealing my self-fulfilling prophesy. Impossible. I take the plate, handed a bat. What the fuck is this thing? I haven't touched one in thirty-five years. Wobbly, I assume the position, bat at the ready. Steve on the mound before me. I give him a smile, hoping he'd take pity and lob me an easy gift. Not Steve, ever super competitive. He stands stone faced. Me, face cold white. He pitches. Fast. Hard. Time stands still. The ball moves towards me, slow motion. Enters my strike zone. I hopelessly swing. *THWACK!!!* The heavens open as a long high ball flies out of the field, disappearing in the park forest. Astonished, I take off, as does our guy on second. He comes home scoring, me farther behind. No matter. Final score four to three. What? Don't ask me.

My team douses me with beer, hoisting me on their shoulders, chanting, "Mick! Mick! Mick! My heart explodes with joyous relief. Steve shakes my hand smiling.

"Wrong Way Benderoth," the albatross round my neck, gone forever. A sports hero.

Sports…take 'em or leave 'em…take 'em…sort of.

Icehouse

Saturday is movie day at The Waverly Theater. Double feature, and a serial. "War of the Worlds," the original, plus..." The Wolfman," a Universal classic, 1944. Lon Chaney Jr, not his dad, but make-up saves his butt. The serial, "Rocket Man," final chapter. Steve, 8 and me, 10, were psyched. After the flicks, White Castle burgers, small freshly baked buns, onions grilled with the fresh ground beef...ten cents. We always buy four each.

Steve looking at his beloved "Howdy Doody" wristwatch, "We're late. Let's take the short cut behind the alley past the icehouse."

Me, "I hate going by that creepy place." It was ancient, delipidated, some say haunted, long abandoned since fridges took over.

From out of nowhere, three teen age street characters block our way. One curly haired blond, the tallest, one oily black hair, badly in need of a barber, number three, burley, with a crew cut.

Curly, menacing, "How much, you got? Money, how much?"

Steve, cautiously, "We're late for a movie. Get out of our way."

Crewcut drifts behind us. Black Hair, "Smart ass punk, he's little. I'll take him."

Me, forcefully, "You touch him and I'll..."

31

Curly pulls out a knife, "You wanna get cut? Terrified, surrounded, they close in. Crewcut grabs me, I struggle, he raps me on the ear, hard.

Black Hair grabs Steve, "Help! Help! Somebody. Help!"

Curly, "Scream all you want, pissant, ain't nobody here...but us." He frisks me, takes my dollar. Black Hair gets Steve's bill, and wrestles off his prized wristwatch.

Steve, "Gimmie that back."

Curly, waving his knife, "You don't wanna get stuck, shut up."

Me, bravely, "You got our money. Let us go."

Curly licks his bottom lip, "We got other plans." He nods to his boys. They drag us struggling toward the icehouse. Curly lifts two loose boards. They strong arm us inside. The boards clap shut, the only daylight piercing the cracks, blinding white slats on the walls. They shove us deeper inside, against a moldy gate.

Curly unzips his fly, pulls out his hard penis and slinks over to Steve, "Get down on your knees and suck me...suck my dick."

Steve frantically, "No!"

Curly, closer, "Suck it, or we'll drop you...down there," pointing to a gaping hole in the icehouse floor.

Black Hair forces Steve to the hole, pushes him to the edge. Harrowing. A rusted ice shoot vanishing into darkness. Black Hair kicks Steve's feet from under him, holds him by his wrists, dangles him over the chute. Me, powerless.

Curly to Steve, "You gonna blow me, or you wanna get dropped."

Steve, blanched, silent, frozen.

Crewcut laughs, loosens his grip on me.

I break away, bust through the loose boards, running, powered by adrenalin, fast...faster...fastest. Down the alley onto Greenmount Avenue, "Hell, Help, police!" I scream.

People stop, stare, turn away, move on. People. I see an open door in a bar.

I run in, up to the bartender gasping for air, "I need help. Three guys have my little brother in the icehouse. Gonna drop him down the shut if he doesn't do stuff to them."

Bartender, "What kind of stuff?"

"I point to my fly, "Stuff, you know," touching my fly, "This stuff."

The bartender nods toward two guys on stools, "Let's go! They reach the icehouse ahead of me. I catch up. Show them the hanging boards. We go inside. Curly, Black Hair and Crewcut are gone. Steve is whimpering on the floor.

The bartender gently lifts Steve onto his feet. "Did you do anything...to them?" Steve shakes his head, "No, but they tried to. He took out his, his...I kicked at it. They laughed. Heard a car coming down the alley. Dropped me and ran out." "Are you ok?" Steve nods yes.

Bartender, turns to me, "What did they look like?" I describe them, every detail...the knife.

Bartender, "Than damn Robbie Strang and those punks he hangs with, all trouble. Where do you boys live?"

"Whitridge Avenue, 410," Steve sobs.

Stool guy one, "I live across twenty eighth, I know Whitridge. I'll take them home." To the bartender, "Frankie, you find Sergeant Hilner, you know his beat. Tell him to call it in."

Back home, safe, I choke, tremble, telling Mom our horror story. She cuddles Steve in her arms, wiping away his flood of tears with a Kleenex. "It's ok, Stevie. It's all over. You'll never have to see them again. I wish that were true. Mom calls Dad. It's dark now. Dad comes home. We're timid telling him our ordeal. He's often quick to blame us for situations not our fault.

Dad, explosively, "Why the hell did you go down that alley in the first place!"

33

Mom, cautiously, "Ben."

Dad, furious…at us. "Why the hell don't you ever listen to what I tell you? You ask for trouble. You get it." We are now the enemy. We don't answer knowing "back talk" would stoke his temper even more.

A phone call, the police. They've rounded up the boys and want me and Steve to identify them. Dad silently, grim faced drives us to the station.

Outside, lined up in front, Curly, Black Hair, and Crewcut, a cop on each side.

Dad gets out of the car, "Is that them?" We nod yes. "Stay inside," he grunts. We are more than happy to.

Dad and the cops talk. We can't hear. The cop nods… releasing the gang. He let these monsters go. They sink into the night. Dad gets back inside the car.

Me, astonished, "It …it was them. Why did the police let them go?"

Dad, "Ah, just a bunch of teenagers, fooling around. Never been arrested. they learned their lesson."

Steve, "Did you get my watch?"

Dad, "I forgot to ask. Get another one."

Steve, "It…it was special. My "Howdy Doody" Grandpa gave it to me. My first watch."

Dad, "Whatever. What's done is done."

Steve and I face each other in shock, disbelief. Our father let us down…again. I filed it in my head with other mounting grievances, never brought to light, fearing his temper when crossed. The icehouse, chilling end to the start of a perfect day.

Callinectes sapidus

Rock Creek, a cove on the shores of the Chesapeake Bay. A perfect spot for a summer house. Nothing fancy. Tiny everything; kitchen, three bedrooms, and a screened in porch to keep out the bat-sized mosquitos that swarmed at dusk. To my younger brother Stevie and I it was heaven.

A long pier jutted out into the water, tailor made for running and diving into the warm brackish back bay water, full of *blue crabs*, a Maryland delicacy when steamed with spicy Old Bay seasoning. These crustaceans, genus and species name, *"Callinectes sapidus," meaning beautiful swimmers,* sped backwards through the water, using their back fins like helicopter props.

To catch crabs, we fished for slimy eels that we packed in coffee cans filled with coarse salt. When they dried out, we tied chunks on long strings, threw the baited end in the water, and waited for the critters to grab on tight with their treacherous claws. Then, ever so slowly, pulled in the string, expertly scooping up the crabs with a long-handled net.

I was taking home movies of Steve kneeling on the edge of the pier crabbing. He has a heavy one on the line, coaxing it in inch by inch. Cousin Billy standing by, net ready. Steve so into catching this sucker, he leans over too far, falling ass over tin cups into the drink. I keep filming. He surfaces, sees me, and yells red faced for me to stop. I get it all on film. Now on the family gag reel. History.

Our extended family descended on our shore house every weekend they could finagle. Free beer. Free crabs. Steve and I crabbed all morning so we could harvest enough for another Maryland tradition, "The Crab Feast." Our bounty, piled steaming hot on a picnic table covered with newspaper, signaled ravenous Marylanders to attack the crabs with wooden mallets. The only way to get the succulent meat within. Beer for the adults, Pepsi for the kids.

This revelry went on for hours, until there was nothing left but a heap of empty shells, which were rolled up in the newspaper and shoved into a galvanized trash can. Then, hands covered with Old Bay, the sated crowd dashed into the water to wash, then play water tag until the mosquitoes came out, chasing us inside the screened-in porch, where the kids slurped popsicles and the grownups watched The Milton Berle Show on a seven-inch black and white TV.

At every crab feast, family members called out to see the movie of Steve's unexpected crab plunge. Off the pier. He made me promise, "Scouts Honor," never to show the film, but always did, leaving my family in hysterics and Steve humiliated, shaking his fist, as he clumped up the club room stairs and slammed the door. Forever a crabby kid.

Gone Fishing

A perfect morning. Sunny, warm, no wind, calm surf. Steve and I planned this trip for a month.

"Hurry up, untie the ropes, I'll pull the boat up on the beach," I commanded. I always ordered him around. I was the older brother. I relished the position of power. He balked. I told him to button it. I was his big brother, in charge. I put the fishing gear in the boat as Mom brought a cooler of lunch.

I pushed off.

Mom waved goodbye, yelling, "Good luck!"

We were on our way. As usual, I was at the wheel.

"Why do you always steer?"

"Because I know the way."

"But I'm a better driver."

"You crashed the pier last week, remember. Cost Dad to have the hole in the bow repaired."

Steve resentfully took his usual second place seat at the stern.

My plan was ambitious. A ten-mile ride to the best striped bass fishing on the bay. I had borrowed an extra fuel tank from our next-door neighbor. It would take one tank to get there, one to get back.

Two hours later we were just off the Southern shore of the awesome Chesapeake Bay Bridge. I picked a spot and tied the anchor rope to the eye hook outside the stern. I took out my trusty Kodak Brownie home movie camera and shot the magnificent glittering span of the newly finished bridge

41

connecting Maryland's eastern and western shores, eliminating the historic ferry between two shores.

We fished hard for two hours. Nothing. Clouds started covering the sun, a slight blew up. Bored, I lounged on the deck. Steve laid over the seats. I dozed off.

Then, "Mickey! Mickey!"

I jumped up! The wind was heavier. White caps slapped the water. All Steve had to do was point. Waves splashed over the stern. Hard rain. A squall. Rule number one: Call the weather before you take a boat trip. Rule number two: Never anchor a boat from the stern. These lessons were hard learned.

"Untie the anchor," I ordered.

Steve leaned over. "I can't reach it." Three footers crashed over his head.

"Get out of the way. I'll do it." I jumped to the back. Big mistake. Our combined weight submerged the stern. That was all she wrote. As the boat filled with water I watched in horror as my Kodak Brownie home movie camera slid off the seat sinking to the bottom of the bow. Panic set in. Helpless, we froze as the boat flipped over, throwing us into the bay. Dazed, I watched the boat sink. The life preservers floated away. Nearest beach, five miles.

"We have to swim for it," I said.

We swam for hours against the tide until I was exhausted. I floated helplessly in the water.

"Come on," Steve called.

"I can't make it," I gasped.

"You have to!" Steve pivoted and swam up to me. "Hold on to my shoulders."

"We'll both go down," I whimpered.

"Just hold on."

I put my arms around his neck. Steve swam for both of us.

Hours later he yelled "Put your feet down!"

"What?" I gurgled.

"We're on a sand bar. Put your feet down! We have a ways to go."

I put my feet down. They touched bottom. I stood up. Exhausted, we treaded against the breakers, but we made it, flopping like dead fish on the deserted beach.

Out of nowhere an elderly black man limped over. "I saw you all out there. I can't swim so I called the cops."

Steve struggled to regain his breath, "Thank you so much, sir. We had a...."

Man, smiling kindly, "I saw that. Prayed for you."

I was too played out to utter a word.

The police drove up in a few minutes, drove us home, our prized boat on the bottom of the bay, my prized movie camera was history.

I could have cared less. All I knew was Steve had saved my life. I never thought of him as *little brother* again.

Jazz

I remember Atlantic City, way, way before the casinos. The boardwalk was our summer wonderland.

Tacky souvenir shops, fresh-squeezed orange juice stands, Thresher's French fry booths, lined the weathered wooden walkway. AC's main boardwalk attraction, The Steel Pier, a magic realm lined with arcades, leading finally to the awesome Diving Bell. My brother Steve and I dreamed of plunging down under the ocean. Our family came here for two weeks every summer. Steve and I were in heaven, long days on the beach, swimming in the frigid ocean, nights cruising the boardwalk, ending up at the Steel Pier.

By afternoon the boardwalk was scorching. Bare feet on fire, Steve and I ran top speed, racing down to the even hotter sand, finally reaching the shade of our beach umbrella. I was not a sun worshiper like my brother. Basted with Johnson & Johnson baby oil cut with iodine, Steve was getting fried crisp under the blazing sun.

Blazing sun. Steve and I way over excited. We were finally going to The Steel Pier. Unfortunately, he got a blistering neon red sunburn that even Noxzema couldn't ease. So, I went alone.

I weaved through the crowds heading for my destination, a novelty shop with awesome gadgets every boy coveted. Strains of unfamiliar music filtered its way through the cacophonous crowd. Being a drummer and electric bass player,

I instinctively followed the trail to the source, winding up at the Steel Pier bandstand.

I saw five jazz musicians on stage wearing black suits and tie. The front man blowing on his trumpet. The rest of the band creating this wild melodic sound—hot drummer, upright bass player, tenor sax, alto sax, trombone, and piano. In an eye blink, the trumpet player moved stage front for his solo. He blew me away. A banner over his head, The Maynard Ferguson Band.

Suddenly, a hand tapped my shoulder. I turned to see Cindy Ferguson, a girl in my 10th grade homeroom.

We yelled in unison over the music, "Cindy!" "Mick!"

"What a cool surprise," she said. "Here to catch the band?"

"I heard the music, wanted to see where it came from. Definitely not rock and roll," I added.

"Jazz!," popped Cindy. "Cool, cool Jazz."

At school, Cindy's outfits, changed colors daily. She wore black tights, a shockingly colored tank top, a short, short skirt, and high-top red sneakers. Her family had moved to Baltimore from New York City's Greenwich Village because her father, an orchestra conductor, was hired to work with The Baltimore Symphony. Her mom was a singer on TV commercials. They were known to be free thinking, liberal intellectuals.

Cindy's eclectic style made the other girls uncomfortable. They giggled as she passed by in the hall. I was intrigued and wanted to get to know Cindy. She showed up solo at school hops, where my band, The Centaurs, blasted out rock and roll. She danced by herself, with captivating free form movements. Everybody else was doing a jerky version of Chubby Checkers' "The Twist."

Maynard Ferguson's solo echoed through the pier, jazz, yeah, jazz, I thought. Knew about it, never explored it.

"What brings you here?" I asked Cindy.

"Maynard's my uncle," she said proudly. "Maynard Ferguson, Cindy Ferguson, Ferguson, Ferguson, get it? What do you think?"

"Well, he's…he's…"

"A hip cat," she touted. "The coolest trumpet man to crash the scene. Want to meet him? He's ending the set and coming over to my dad and mom's apartment for a party, you can come."

I considered the invite for a millisecond, "Yes, absolutely."

The band finished with a powerful flourish, earning loud cheers, and applause from the adoring crowd.

"Come with me," Cindy ordered. Before I could say a thing, she took my hand and yanked me backstage. The band was packing up. Maynard was draining his trumpet.

"Hey Maynard," she called.

He looked up, smiling lovingly "Babes! You made it. Like the set?"

"Outrageous. Way, way cool. I want you to meet a guy I go to school with, he's a rock drummer."

"R & R," Maynard smiled. "Chuck Berry's *The Man,* Johnny B. Goode, my fav, play it?"

"Yes sir," I replied.

"Not 'Sir', just Maynard. And you?"

"Mick," I replied.

He held out his hand, we shook.

"Let's move, kids. Don't want the party starting without us."

I realized I had never let go of Cindy's hand. I felt secure, nice. The three of us raced off the board walk to Maynard's awesome red Corvette, no hood, chrome air filters blasting up. My eyes popped. 'Way cool,' I thought. This night was getting more and more outrageous.

Maynard's Corvette screamed as he pulled up to an upscale Atlantic City condo complex. Revs the Vette's motor, *Baroom! Baroom! Baroom!* Shuts his monster off.

"Here we are, kiddies. Time to play."

We jumped out, ran up to the building. Security Guard knows this famous man. Nods, smiles, high fives Maynard.

"Mr. F. Glad to see ya again."

We took the elevator to the penthouse, door wide open, party in full swing. Maynard's jazz recordings in the background. Cindy hauled me over to a couple. The man wore a tux up top and star-studded Bermudas on the bottom, leather thongs on his feet. The woman had on a bikini top and a floor length silk skirt to match.

"Mick, meet my parents, Maggie and James." She called her parents by their first names? Whoa, I was on a different planet entirely.

"Hi Mick," said James.

"Charmed," said Maggie.

"Mick's a schoolmate, hooked up at Maynard's gig," Cindy said.

"Make yourself comfy," said Maggie. "Buffet's in dining room, bar's in the kitchen."

"Nice to meet...," I started but didn't get a chance to finish.

Cindy showed me into the kitchen where some guy, tie undone, was using a blender.

"Max, Mick, Mick, Max. Maynard's alto sax," Cindy grinned.

"Margaritas good for you two?" he asked.

"Excellent," Cindy said.

Max rimmed two Champaign glasses with salt and poured the drinks. "Cuervo Tequila, fresh lime juice and triple sec, you'll love it," Max replied.

I leaned closer to Cindy and whispered, "Your parents let you drink?"

"Not really, but this is a special occasion, so we're sneaking a bit." She held up two frosty glasses, handing one to me. "To us," Cindy cheered.

We toasted and sipped. Bang! De-frigging-licious.

"Like it?"

"It's ...it's great."

"Drink it slow" she warned, "Tequila packs a kick."

We walked into the crowded living room. My glass empty, I was feeling no pain. I glanced at my watch. 11:30, my parents would be worried.

"I better get home."

"Past your bedtime?" Cindy joked. "Come on, I'll walk ya."

We wobbled along I felt Cindy almost carried me along talking nonstop. I don't remember a word she said except, "Here chew this." Handing me two sticks of Wrigley's peppermint. "Don't want the folkies smellin' the booze."

I chewed, we walked, she talked. It was like a dream. I never felt better in my life. When I spotted my parent's cottage I had to shape up quick.

"I had a great...cool, time, Cindy, thanks."

"The pleasure was all mine."

"Maybe I'll see you tomorrow," I said.

"Leaving early in the morning," she pouted.

Spontaneously, Cindy stood on tiptoe and kissed me lightly on the lips. A quick peck but more than friendly. She turned, starting to walk away.

"See you in school. Maybe we'll be together in homeroom again. If not, I'll find you," she called.

I stood for a time, watching her saunter away. Cindy Ferguson. A true original. She was...she was...JAZZ!

Gem

Uncommonly sophisticated for a high school senior, Deborah Kushner was called Gem by her conservative Jewish family. She was a Milford Mill High School honor student, star of Milford's renowned drama department. She landed leads in musicals "Bye, Bye Birdie," "Kiss Me Kate," and "Annie Get Your Gun." Deborah inherited a unique, captivating vocal style from her cantor father. I didn't know what a Cantor was. I was a Gentile. Different worlds.

Stardom has a price. Affable, outgoing, popular with a few Jewish girls, Deborah had no boyfriends. Boys looked at her with awe, but from a safe distance, afraid of her stellar mantle. Gentile girls shied away, unable to comprehend this self-assured, ephemeral creature. Debby was impossibly out of my league, me being a *goy*. Fantasies would have to suffice.

I was popular with my own crowd, a senior with a wry sense of humor, and a hot, flashy drummer in the awesome rock band, The Centaurs. I had a flock of girlfriends, groupies, nothing serious.

Deborah and I often crossed paths as members of the drama club. Occasionally we'd chat. She was one of the few who got my off-center jests, poking me, laughing, "Oh, You," her coveted reply, whirling away, an intoxicating fragrance trailing. The nearness of Deborah excited me. Too bad. Different worlds…again.

Summertime, 1963, end of the year. Electric excitement. Finals, term papers, graduation… The Senior Prom.

I was way behind on schoolwork, the band flooded with gigs. First things first.

Packing up our equipment after a frat dance, my brother Steve, asks. "Who's the lucky girl this year, Mick?"

"Girl? What girl?" I huffed, hoisting my kick drum, The Centaurs logo on the front head.

"The Prom, Senior prom, ditz. Who's your date?"

Holy shit! So deluged with band jobs and school catch up, I forgot to get a date for the prom. I panic. Frantic, I call my groupies, one after another. Zilch. Already taken by my smirking band mates. No date, no prom, self-image, demolished.

Then "it" happens, out of the blue. I see Deborah Kushner, struggling with her locker. I approach, "Need help?"

"Oh, Mick, the door's jammed and my father's waiting to pick me up for Friday night services."

"Let me try." She backs away. I size up the problem, rusty bent hinges. I pull with unknown strength, ripping the door off, surprising both of us. We burst out laughing.

"Well, at least it's opened," she beams. "Lucky you happened by. Thanks so much, Macho Mick." Smiling her killer smile, she scurries away.

Deborah Kushner? Macho Mick? A side of me I never envisioned. She's halfway down the steps.

Primal courage surges. I yell, "Deborah! Deborah!" My call reverberating down the hall. She stops, turns. More courage, "Do you have a date for the prom?"

Calling back, "No, no I don't. Well not yet," she says coyly.

Deborah. Coy? Whoa, another side.

"Would you, like to go with me?"

"Why, yes, yes, of course I would, but I…I have to ask my father. He's…"

"I understand," I nod.

"You do?"

"Yes, I do."

"That's so thoughtful. Can I let you know on Monday?"

"Absolutely."

"I'll find you. Thanks for asking me."

"My pleasure," bowing a bit.

She returns a modest curtsy. "Till Monday."

Deborah Kushner turns, disappears out the door.

Dazed. Did this just happen? Yes, it did. Different worlds...hopeful.

Saturday night. A huge, high-paying gig, University of Maryland, Phi Delta Phi, end of the term bash. I'm loading my kit in the van.

My mother leans out the front door, "Mick! Mick! A phone call. A girl, Deborah something."

Not something...Kushner. Deborah Kushner. Calling me?

"I'll...I'll take it in the club room."

"Hurry up, man," Steve barks. "The guys are waiting. Bring up the mic case. I left it down there somewhere."

Somewhere. I could give a darn. Backyard lights out, I grope through the darkness, find the steps to the clubroom. Inside, I trip over the friggin' mic case, vault for the phone, pulling it down to the floor with me.

Breathless, I answer the phone, "Hello?"

"It's me, Deborah. Guess what? Lucky us. My father said yes."

'Lucky us.' Did Deborah Kushner say, 'Lucky us?' Lucky me.

On the floor, tangled in a coiled phone cord... "Great, great, really...great." Is that the only word I know?

Deborah, excited, "I couldn't wait until Monday. I got your number off one of your band cards."

Deborah had one of our band cards? Worlds nearer?

She says, "The Centaurs, part man, part horse, cool."

57

Cool? Did Deborah Kushner actually say cool? Mindboggling.

"Thanks for calling, Deborah."

"Call me Gem, my family does."

Gem? Gem? Spellbound.

"See you Monday, Mick."

"Bye…Gem." Click. Entranced. Two worlds coming together.

Buffed that my dad let me use his pride and joy, a bright yellow Pontiac Bonneville convertible. I park in front of the Kushner house, a three-level modern, new. All of the suburban houses were new.

Front door, frosted glass, engraved, floral pattern. Me, rented tux, corsage box in hand, shivering. It's eighty degrees. I lean to press the bell, never make it. Door swings open, backlit, dim silhouette. Mr. Kushner, tall, thin, three piece tailored black suit, black tie. A hand gesture beckons me in. I go. Living room, patterned rugs, light wood floors, black leather couch, embroidered armchairs, paintings, faded old world photos adorn the walls. Standout, a long wooden hand railed staircase ascending to a landing, a portrait of Gem on the wall. Another planet.

Mr. Kushner approaches. I dry my wet palm against my tux coat.

"Mick, right?"

I nod, "Yes, sir, Mick Benderoth." We shake. His hand, dry warm, firm. Mine, a sponge.

"Gem's told us much about you. A musician?"

"Yes, sir."

"Music, my third love, after Mrs. Kushner," pointing to his wife, then up to the portrait, "And Gem."

Mrs. Kushner, again tall, svelte, in a white linen suit, beige blouse, string of pearls, a sizable diamond ring. She smiles, speaks in a soft, clear voice. Takes my hand. Drier this time.

"You've known each other since seventh grade, yes?"

58

"In the same class, junior and senior high."

"In drama club."

"Bit parts for me. Backstage crew a lot."

"All important parts of the company. Let me buzz Gem." She picks up a white phone, presses one of six clear plastic buttons. It lights. Intercom. You're not in Kansas anymore, Mickey.

"Gem, Mick is here. Yes. Fine." She hangs up. "She's on her way.

Gem appears on the landing, momentarily obscuring her portrait. She descends, revealing the painting as if she stepped out of it. Two Gems. Forever emblazed.

Her strapless, sky-blue gown, matching heels, a modest, sleek tiara adorns her hair. I have no words. Our eyes meet. Walking directly to me grinning, she straightens my tie, sliding her fingers down my lapels.

"Very elegant," Gem says.

Me, from nowhere, "You, Gem...beyond words."

"So poetic. Thank you, Mickey."

I shakily hold out the corsage box. She opens it.

"Orchids, look Mother, Cymbidiums, our favorite."

My junior prom date, a nosegay, no treacherous pin. Mrs. Kushner senses my unease, comes to my rescue, effortlessly pinning the corsage beneath Gem's naked shoulder.

"Exquisite," Gem's mom says.

"Yes," I say, "From head to toe." Where did that come from? They laugh. Accepting? Time to go.

The Prom at The Randallwood, a lavish pavilion for weddings, birthdays, bar and bat mitzvahs. The Centaurs often gigged here.

The dance floor, filled with the Class of 1963, tuxed and gowned. On stage, a classy club quintet plays pop standards. Gem and I enter arm in arm. Heads turn. Eyes widen. Tongues buzz. We are saved by my band mates. I introduce Gem. Her strong, melodious voice conquers. the din.

59

Gem, "Nice to meet all of you! Hope to hear you play someday!"

The prom combo plays a personal favorite, "I Love Paris." The Centaurs play it too…a very different version.

I take Gem's hand, "Shall we?"

"Love too." Gem, in my arms, respectful distance. A Gem smile, she pulls in closer. "You know, this is my first school dance. My father…"

"Glad he made an exception."

"As am I."

We swirl all night, kids warm up, socialize, like teenagers. Gem is all mine…for one night.

We drive back to her house, Bonneville top down. Gem's gorgeous head wrapped in her white chiffon scarf blowin' in the wind.

She laughs, "I've never been in a convertible. It's fun. So cool."

Me thinking, 'Cool, Gem said cool. Bliss.'

Gem, this is all so exciting. Thanks for asking me My Macho Mick.

Me joyous musing again, 'My Macho Mick this time. I'm Deborah Kushner's Macho Mick. It don't get no better than this. Driving a hot car with my dream girl. King of the world.'

Gem, "I hope we can do this again."

Me, at a loss for words. I squeal the Bonneville up to her house.

Gem, "You're a real hot rod."

Hot rod. Macho. Me. I hop out driver's side, rush to open the car door for her. We walk up and stand on her front porch.

"I had the most wonderful time. So comfortable being with you, meeting The Centaurs. Thanks Mick." She leans close.

I hope for lips, she turns to my cheek, a sweet peck. No romance, a newfound dear friend.

"Goodnight Macho. See you Monday."

"Goodnight, Gem." I'm…I'm…I'm…spellbound.

Next weekend, another prize gig. University of Maryland graduation dance. I take a chance. Call Gem. Get her father, "Just a moment, I'll buzz her."

Music. "Mick, nice to hear your voice," she says.

"Same here. Band has a gig. Saturday night. Hope you can come."

"Mick, the prom was a special occasion. I'd really love to, but I know what my father will say."

"I sort of thought…."

"But if he doesn't know…"

"What?"

"You know Mandel's Deli?"

"Liberty Road strip mall."

"What time's the gig."

"Starts at nine. Forty-five minutes to get there."

"Pick me up at 7:30."

"Gem…are you sure?"

"Very."

"Ok, then."

"See you. Bye-bye."

Click. Worlds collide. Yes!

The U of M gymnasium is mobbed. The guys set up.

Katelin Parker, Steve's long-time girlfriend, a bubbly sweetheart, bounces up to Gem. "Hi, Deborah, I'm Katelin."

Deborah to Katelin, "Call me Gem."

Katelin, "Ok, Gem it is. Let's stand up front."

Gem looks at me on the bandstand. Does a shy wave, follows Katelin.

I wait for Steve's downbeat, on stage, secure behind my drums,. We launch into our opener, Ray Charles classic, "What'd I Say." We cook. The crowd rocks. I look out, spot Katelin and Gem dancing. Awesome, Gem under a rock and roll spell. We finish the set. The guy's head straight for the bar, free beer.

I rush to Gem, "Having fun?"

"You guys are fantastic. I love it."

The band, frosty beers in hand gather round.

Gem asks, "Do you guys know, "It's My Party," by Leslie Gore?"

Steve, ever the fearless leader, "Know it, never played it, why?"

"I was just wondering if…I could sing?"

Woah mamma!

Steve, "Sure. We'll follow your lead."

Gem, "Cool." …again.

Steve bows to her, ladies first. Gem takes the stage. We follow, drift into place.

Steve leans to the mic, his smooth deejay voice floats over our P.A., "Attention, Ladies and Gentlemen." All face the stage. Steve, croons, "A very, very special quest tonight, presenting…Gem." Steve steps back.

Gem at stage front faces Steve, nodding as she knowingly counts off. The band is hers. She pulls the mic off its stand. Takes over the stage, struts, instinctual moves…a star, Leslie Gore's hit, Gem style.

"It's my party, and I'll cry if I want to, cry if I want to, cry if I want to. You would cry too if it happened to you!"

The crowd stops dancing, everyone faces Gem, clapping in rhythm, singing along. Musical magic. Finishing to cheering applause, beaming, Gem curtsies, new fans, turns to me, flashing that signature smile…blows me a kiss.

Ecstatic memory. One world.

Jimi Hendrix

Dear Jimi Hendrix,

I want to bless you for the memorable Christmas you gave me, December,1967. I bow at your altar, indebted forever...but before you make your awesome appearance, indulge me...a little history first. So light up, lay back, and play a riff or two. Background music.

My brother, Steve and I were joined at the hip, thick as thieves, a brotherly bond it later took an emotional earthquake to break, a super glue part of that bond, rock and roll. We formed and played in bands from elementary through high school. Me, the drummer, Steve the bass player. Eight glorious years, put on hold by college.

Steve went to Carnegie Mellon to major in drama, dreaming of acting on Broadway, or Hollywood movies. I chose Albright College, a small school known for its pre-med curriculum. I dreamed of becoming a doctor.

It was nineteen sixty-seven, we were coming home for Christmas break. I drove to Baltimore's Penn Station to pick Steve up. At first, I didn't recognize him. All I saw was this tall guy with shoulder length hair, black pirate shirt, chartreuse vest, striped bell bellbottom pants and leather Indian moccasins. I was wearing a grey suit, white shirt and skinny tie and brown brogues.

This was clearly the beginning of a major sea change. Little did I realize then that Steve was my Christmas present. Needless to say, Mom and Dad were speechless when Steve appeared in the front doorway. Enough about parents.

It was December 23, a date now emblazoned in my mind. Mom and Dad were at an office Christmas soiree, Steve and I jamming in our club room...a holy place where many of our bands had lived and died.

This is where you come in, Jimi.

Steve put down his bass and reached in its case. "Got an early present for you."

He pulled out a flat package that could only have been a record album. I was excited to find out what he was into. I unwrapped it to see a picture of a trio dressed just like Steve. In the center, a gorgeous black man with a cool Afro, bookended by two longhaired white guys leaning on his shoulders, the title, *Are You Experienced?*"

"This guy will blow your mind," Steve smiled devilishly. "JIMI HENDRIX."

Blow my mind? What the hell did that mean?

"Who is he?" I asked, way out of touch.

"We'll get to that. Just listen." He gently set down the needle. A moment of silence... then... YANNNGGGGANGGNE!!!! A cacophonous sound imploded my eardrums. The most horrible music, if it was music, I ever heard.

"Turn it down!," I shouted.

"Meant to be listened to loud!" he yelled.

I loved soul music, the blues, Motown, Chuck Berry, James Brown. We played all of it. I knew that without black music, there would be no rock and roll. But this...this...what the hell was this?

"Please, Steve, turn it down."

Instead, he slowly turned it off. Another moment of silence.

"Here, let's try this," Steve said calmly, knowingly.

He pulled a plastic baggie from his vest pocket. Opened it, showed it to me. A bag of dried sticks and weeds. Where is this going?

66

"Grass," was all he said.

Marijuana, grass, weed. Illegal shit. Against the law. I start to freak. He slips out a packet of rolling papers. I watched nervously as he expertly cleaned the grass on the Jimi Hendrix album cover, rolling the seeds free from the brown weeds. Then sprinkling the stuff in a folded rolling paper, licking the top, and twisting it closed.

"A joint," holding it up. "We should let it dry for a sec."

With that, he put the joint between his lips and magically flicked a barn burner match with his thumb, lit the end, inhaled deeply, held his breath, exhaled slowly. A cloud of smoke circled his face. He passed it to me.

"Now…you bro."

Me…bro? Ok…ok. I did what I was told, I took the joint, sucked it in, and coughed it out violently.

"Easy, easy, now pay attention. Slowly fill your mouth with smoke, gently take it into your lungs, hold it in for 30 seconds. Exhale. You'll get the hang of it."

We passed the joint back and forth talking and laughing a long, long, long time. Then, Steve says "Now, let's listen to Jimi again."

I did. That was that. Jimi, I'm now seventy-five. You and my brother Steve are jamming somewhere in rock heaven. I listen to you every day, iPhone, computer, my maxed-out stereo. Your mind-blowing licks still flood me with vivid images of the first time my bro turned me on to you and weed. Now "Manic Depression" blasts out of my Jensen speakers in the background.

Thanks, Jimi. Thank you so, so much. You blew open my mind. A new me.

Much more than fondly,

Mick Benderoth

Progeny

Young people" the future of humankind... and their planet. Teaching them, taught me... to listen, to learn.

My father pulled strings to get me a job in a Baltimore Jr. high, so I could beat the Vietnam draft. Teachers were deferred.

I went to college to become a doctor, not a teacher, but I had enough biology and chemistry credits to qualify to teach science. I thought teaching would be a lark, an easy way to avoid the war. Naive yes, out of touch, yes... way, way, way wrong, yes, yes, and yes. It was the hardest job I've ever had.

I was clueless when I walked into the classroom my first day. I was late. A torrential downpour flooded the highways. Drenched, water running down matted hair, I slumped into the room, a drowned new teacher. Silence.

The school principal, Charlie Benson, a kind, understanding man, was watching my class until I showed up.

He leaned in, whispering, "You ok, Mick? Heck of a storm. I was worried." I nodded yes.

Charlie patted my back, smiling, "They're all yours, teach," then left me, dripping, in front of a room full of seventh graders. The savviest young people on earth.

My mind raced. How can I change their first impression of me as a late, wet newbie. Desperate, I grabbed the class roster and began rattling off their names, right or wrong, top speed. They started giggling, then bursting out laughing.

After I finished, I said "Glad to meet y'all... and who am I?"

I wrote my name in huge letters on the blackboard. "Mr. Benderoth. Tough name. Don't bother," I smiled, "Mr. B. is just fine." And that's who I became for four years, Mr. B.

I skipped the usual filing cards with info drill, jumping right into asking their favorite things; foods, games, school subjects, tv shows, music... freewheeling it. They loosened up, we had fun. A one-on-one with a teacher, not about rules, but us. Woah! They raised their hands wildly. We bonded, the bell rang, dismissed, on to their next class, spreading dish about Mr. B.

I respected them as equals, they returned in kind. That's how I taught, they taught back, young people.

Four years flew. I had a hard decision. My supervisors said I was a natural. SoSo, keep teaching? Or leave to follow a dream so crazy it confounded everyone... except me? Go to Hollywood and make movies?

"Think hard about this. You're flushing your future down the toilet," my father growled. "For... for... for what?"

That's where we left it. He didn't know me from Adam.

Flash forward ten years, living in a New York brownstone with Nancy Perl, 13 years my senior with two stepdaughters. Rebecca and Sarah. Street-smart, well-educated, private schooled, privileged, but they had the same fears and aspirations as my Jr. High students. Becky, Sarah, and I became fast friends, equals. It lasts to this day. They teach. I keep learning. Young people.

Flash forward ten more years. Becky and Sarah in Ivy League colleges, me, back from Hollywood, recovering from burn out, making commercials with Nancy in Manhattan, cooling out weekends at the family home in East Hampton.

One sweltering afternoon my wife Nancy is at her painting class at The Barge. She has a show coming up, working 24/7 to get the last of her paintings completed. My little dynamo is always calm, cool, collected. She produces TV commercials for the biggest international companies like Pepsi, Superwoman. Now, not so much. I've never seen her composureless before. Her first show in years. Even an article in the Times. She never fails to rise. Nancy is the rock in our duo. She will prevail victorious.

I'm in my office facing a blank screen, with a blank head. I have a story to finish. not finish, start. Nary an idea in sight. A knock at the door. Saved again. Thank you God. I escape from my office. Go to front door. Open. Surprised to see two young people, late teens, a boy and a girl, sweating from the summer heat.

The young woman looked into my eyes, "Mr. Alexander Benderoth?"

"That'd be me. Can I help y'all?" I asked.

She authoritatively pipes up again, "My name is Greta Hanson, this is Thomas Willams. We are volunteers for Save The Children Foundation."

'Interesting.' I muse, 'Very...very...very.'

"You guys must be melting. Come on in. Chill out and ya'll can call me Mick, all my friends do. Irish nickname."

"Oh, thank God. Air conditioning," Greta wisped, waltzing into the living room.

"Make yourselves comfortable. I'll get you something to drink." Greta plopped into an old, over-stuffed velvet armchair. Thomas onto the couch.

"What can I get you?"

"Water's fine...Mick" says Greta.

"Bubbly or tap with, without ice?" I offer.

"Ice would be great,"

"Tom?"

"The same, Mick," finally speaking.

I served drinks, they settle in. "So, tell me about Save The Children."

Recovering from the heat they came alive, Thomas's turn, his pitch, sincere, basic and direct.

"Children are the future, many, all over the world, living in poverty... even here, inner cities, rural south, no schools, health care, no chance to escape, to dream, to excel."

He knocked me out, I'm hooked from the get-go.

"What made ya'll decide to canvas for Save the Children?"

Greta jumped in, "You only have one life. You must use the time you have to bring some good into the world."

I was stunned by this wisdom coming from such a young woman. Literally blown away, I signed up on the spot.

Greta, in charge, "You'll be getting a call from Lynn Baxter, head of the STC central office. He will discuss your sponsorship, help you to choose the right children for you. All from stricken countries who need your help most."

We chatted for a while. Greta handed me the STC brochures, said they had to move on, had a lot of ground to cover.

I gave them each a bottle of cold water.

Greta surprised me with a hug, "Thank you so much."

I shook Thomas's hand. We said goodbye. Excited by their visit I watched these two young people dash off.

I didn't wait for Lynn Baxter to call. I dialed the number on brochure that minute. She was sincerely happy to get my call. I made it a point to mention Greta and Thomas, how they enlightened me with their zeal.

Lynn recommended several of the poorest African countries. I chose Uganda and Somalia. I have Jasu and Falah from Uganda, Guna and Atsha from Somalia. I could send small items, colored pencils, sharpeners, pads, rulers, to the foundation, to be forwarded to my young peoples' villages. We discussed the amount I would donate, whether one time, monthly, or annually. I could call anytime to exit. I never did.

The first thing I got in the mail were photos of Jasu, Falah, Guna, and Atsha. I framed the photos to hang in my office where they still are today.

They sent charming, colorful drawings of their villages and themselves, along with handwritten letters of thanks.

Over the years, I found other young people to sponsor. A gift of continuing fulfillment.

Save The Children. Young people deserve that, and more. Much more.

Living War
Dead

Maxie we called him. Stan Maxwell. Way, way cool for a college freshman. Smoked a pipe and cheap Marsh Wheeling cigars, long and strong. NYC born and bred, family of money and intellects. Private school. A man of privilege with a screw you attitude that only trust funds bring. Introduced me to *The New Yorker.* I read the cartoons, he read the whole thing.

Maxie's liberal politics new to me…any politics were, me a rube from Baltimore suburbs. I sucked him up like a sponge. He wrote editorials to the school newspaper on his fierce protest against the Vietnam war. Never published. Albright College was a church-affiliated school. Right of center. Mandatory weekly chapel. Maxie's never attended.

Didn't give a damn about college, he was slumming. Held court in a hotel bar in downtown Reading, PA. Martinis, hold the veggies, open tab, on him. Maxie's bliss, being a writer. A good one judging by his writing course A's, the only class Maxie attended. He awed me. Sadly, his blasé manner did him in. He skipped his entire sophomore year of classes.. Again, slumming. Junior year, flunked out. Classified 1-A. Drafted. Us bar buddies were horrified. We soon lost contact.

I graduated, taught school for a draft deferment. Planned my first trip to Europe on summer break. Out of the blue, a phone call. Stan Maxie had finished his two-year tour in Nam. Mutual friends told him about my planned trip. They said he needed some serious R&R. He called me. His voice not Maxie's. Someone else, a different Maxie. Asked if we could travel together. Hell yes. Traveling Europe with my college idol. Yes. Yes, again yes. A dream trip.

We meet at the DC airport. I see his long shadow before I see him. I blanche. Maxie's thinner than cool thin. Dour face. Greets unsmiling. No handshake. No trademark hug, nods "Mick."

Me smiling, "Maxie."

Grumbles, "Prefer Stan."

Not the man I worshipped. Not the gregarious raconteur who could keep you enraptured hours. The man now standing before me looked more dead than alive. He slept through the flight to Paris. We were doing the hostel tour. He walked the Paris streets like a ghost. The more we traveled, the less interest he showed in this wonderous, new world we were exploring. I was exploring. His exploring ended in Nam. A dark...dark...darker...black jungle of blood.

His mood starts to bring me down. I'm not having fun at all. I feel like a keeper of a wounded animal. My dream trip, becoming a nightmare. No escape. Me, too guilty to abandon him. Never spoke of his time in hell until one night after a fabulous meal of Coq au Vin Blanc that he did not touch. He started to open. Kept drinking wine. Bottles. I was his crutch, physically, mentally. A caretaker. Arm in arm, we slouched back to our hostel room. He sat on the edge of his bed. Motionless, head bowed for a long, long silence.

Then he began, "Hell is a compliment. War is hell—a joke. Butchery. Both sides. They wanted me to carry a gun. I was a CO, conscientious objector. Named me Peacenik. CO's automatic Medics. In the line of fire, taking care of the wounded, dying, dead. Boys. Not men. We wore helmets, a bright white cross on the front. Medics were VC snipers' prime target. One night my partner and I were pinned down in a deep mud hole. Greg Watson, nice, sweet, guy from Wisconsin, farm boy. We listened to our wounded boys in the tall grass in front wailing in pain, sounds no human was ever meant to make."

He continued, "Guys pleading, 'Medic! Medic! Please dear God, help me!'

We were scared shitless, like every other night. But we had to go out. Greg started to crawl over the edge of the hole first. ZING! PLINK! He fell back into my arms, a bullet hole dead center in his white cross. He was wheezing, barely. His helmet fell off. Brains slid out into my hand. Greg's brains, in my hand. The only reason I didn't vomit, I had vomited out months ago. Greg Watson died. I scraped his brains from my hand, from the edge of his helmet, put it back on what was left of his head. Greg loved Lacrosse. All he talked about."

Stan was somber, glassy-eyed, sat up straight. "Enough for tonight." He passed out on his bed. Never spoke of the war again.

I was traumatized. Unfathomable. Ashamed of my deferment, thankful for it. Our summer holiday jaunt became a bleak series of hostel runs. I was honor-bound to stay with my friend. No escape. Fate smiled. We met two Irish guys our age having a ball hosteling through Europe in a beat up Volks beetle. Raised Irish catholic, I bonded immediately with Taryn and Zeb. They were headed to Scandinavia, Sweden, Denmark. And Amsterdam, my dream city. Invited us to go along.

Stan shook his head. I knew I had no choice but to turn them down. Then he spoke, "Go, Mick. You go. I'll take the ferry back to England. Wait for the plane back. See you then."

How could I leave him alone? But I had to, for my own sanity. In the morning. Maxie surprised me with a spontaneous hug. A long, tight one.

He whispered, "Thanks Mick. For being there."

Tears welled. As my new buds and I pulled away, I saw him grow smaller and smaller…then gone.

The trip turned full face into a riotous party. I took it all in. Good memories. Trip over, I took the Ostend to Dover ferry back to England for the flight home. Maxie was gone. He took a flight back weeks ago. I never heard from him again. Stan Maxwell, Maxie, living war dead.

Promise

Life taunts you with promise.

I was a teacher. Some students showed promise others, not so much. David Anders and Randall Parks were the two most promising high school students I ever taught. Tight friends since middle school. David soft, quiet, sweet, caring, Randall loquacious, mind jumping from one idea to the next, never finishing a thought. Randall's hand was always waving furiously. Sometimes right, sometimes wrong. I had to call on David. Never, ever raised his hand. Always right. David and Randall, one distant, one in your face.

I started an after-school filmmaking club way before it was in vogue. David and Randall shared Randall's uncle's 8mm home movie camera. Of the six students in the club, David was the only one to present a complete film. Randall's attempt was a jumble about his dog, "Snowflake." David's film, "The Future," blew me away, astounding. A well shot, edited collage, graveyards intercut with images of environmental pollution, power company coal-fueled smokestacks blowing black poison over a pristine sunset. Car tailpipes blowing choking exhaust.

David's piece de resistance,? An unexpected music track made on his dad's cassette recorder. Debussy's "Afternoon of the Fawn." Smashing counterpoint. He got it. A natural filmmaker. Speechless, I shook David's hand, smiling proudly. His faint smile back. I arranged for David to show his film at a student council meeting. Students' eyes never left the screen.

They also got it. Way back then. Standing ovation for a masterwork.

David and Randall often visited me during their high school years. Always together. Personalities unchanged, both went to The University of Maryland. Both majoring in theater arts. I lost contact with them, moving from Baltimore to New York City.

Years later I was back in Baltimore for family Christmas. A teacher friend told me Randall was now a rising director in regional theater scene. No news about David. I got tickets to see a play Randall directed. Average, over long, weakly cast, little drama. But he was a working director, but not impressive. We met for drinks after the play. I encouraged him, gave a few positive pointers. I asked him about David.

Randall's face turned white, somber. A long pause. "David committed suicide, hung himself."

I was stunned. Dry mouth. "Why? Why? Why?"

Randall took a long beer pull, a deep breath before responding. "David was gay. I'm the only one who knew. He couldn't come out, deeply depressed, self-shamed, tortured. He called me, the night before. Small talk mostly. He said he was going away. Would keep me posted." Longer pause. "His mother found him in the basement. He'd never left home."

A pall, a last drink. A sad memorial toast for David, a more hopeful one for Randall. Two promising men, one a tragic loss, one a bright future. Said we'd stay in touch, hugged warmly, tearfully.

Years later, my teacher friend sent me a *Baltimore Evening Sun* newspaper clipping. Randall Park's face full front, top of the clip. First I had hopeful thoughts, a rave review of a new play? Not to be. Randall had become a crack addict, in and out of detox, rehab for years. Never shook it. Came home one night, stabbed his wife and mother-in-law to death. Now on death row, awaiting execution.

I'm nauseous. Tears flood my eyes. I imagined Randall and David, star-crossed, sitting in my class, front row.

Life's only promise, no promises.

Shilly

It knocks me for a loop. Living with the love of my life. Lesley Parks, nickname Les, most coveted girl in high school, I won her. Leslie a tall, slender head cheerleader, long blond hair akimbo when flipped in the air landing firmly on both feet, smiling her killer smile. Went to the same collage, Les, one year below me, a knockout there as well. Destined to marry after we both graduated. I did first, teaching school to avoid the Vietnam draft. Got way deep into movie making, my second love, Lesley Parks my primo for sure. Two of my films, festival winners. Who could've wanted more? Bam! Betrayal. Our destinies a trainwreck, a story yet untold. Painful, leaving me shattered, betrayed, heart smashed, … adrift…alone.

Trying to get my mind off myself, a friend drags me to The Maryland Art Fair. "It's a happening," he says, the new word floating in the air. "The coolest of the cool take over the place, artists, musicians, performers it…its…"

"A happening," I grimace.

"Don't be such a wise ass. You might meet…"

"Stop, just stop," I bark.

"Ok, ok, just come."

I sigh, I go. It is a Happening. Carnival atmosphere, hippies mingling with straights. a mélange of cultures, exhilarating, but after a while my doldrums set in, when I hear a voice calling my name.

"Mick, Mick, Benderoth!!" A face from my past. A childhood friend, Steve Yeager. We roller skated up and down the back Baltimore city alley that separated our neighborhoods.

Steve, "Jesus, man is it really you? It's been 15 years." We hug. "What are you up to?"

"Teaching school."

"Holly shit, so am I. To beat the draft?"

"Yup," I quip.

"Still on your way to Hollywood?"

"On the back burner…you?"

"Directing plays, regional theater, rehearsing 'A Thousand Clowns' now," he announces. "Come on by tomorrow night," Steve offered.

I decide to go to Steve's production. I'd seen the Jason Robards movie.

Theater was something I know zilch about. Film was my milieu, but entering the theater, I sensed something unknown to me, live actors on stage. Once you start the show, you can't go back, no editing tricks here. This is real.

Steve's on break, actors mill about. "Hey, you made it, he smiles."

"Whole new world to me," I quip.

Yeager frowns, "Yeah, always another problem to solve. Great play, dream cast, but I'm stuck. A scene where the leads, a young girl and older guy, romp through New York city celebrating their new-found love. Can't get that energy on stage. I'm thinking slide show."

Me, "Slides? Too static. Why not film? Center stage, drop-down screen, music sub plot."

Steve grabs my face, kisses me on the mouth. A hug and a kiss. "You are a genius, just the man to do it. We take the actors to New York City, and you'll film it. Serendipity, you land in my lap, saving my ass after all these years." Another hug.

We do just that. Train to New York. Steve directs, I shoot. We start early, actors holding hands, racing down Fifth Avenue weaving through rush hour throngs. Night, Time Square, decibels pin the meter, neon lights, marquees, hustlers, peddlers, cops on horses, traffic, blaring horns.

New York, New York. Edited to Sinatra's masterpiece, I nail it. Steve gets raves, we get a fond friendship renewed.

One night, tearing down the set, Steve stares at me. "Well…?"

"Well, what?," I ask.

"What's next?"

"Next?" I ask.

"Our next production. We need something unique, off center, shocking." We're in sync. We read over thirty scripts. Nothing. A friend tells Steve about a college professor in Virginia shopping his first play, Preston Lanford. Sources say it's undoable. All Yeager needs to hear. He's out the door, me on his heels.

We visit Lanford's impressive home. He's a tall, conservatively dressed man, soft spoken. "I teach a class at university on racism. I was researching material for a lecture on violence against blacks by whites. I came upon this newspaper story from 1948. I saw the potential for a strong play. Always wanted to try my hand. Once I started writing, I couldn't stop." Preston proudly hands Steve the manuscript, "Willow."

Getting in the car to drive back, Steve commands, "You drive. I read."

He page-turns with a fury. Finishes, turns, smiling devilishly. "Now, I drive, you read."

I see why Langford had no takers, and why Steve grins. Heavy story, dark, raw, and stark. A young black woman is brutally raped by Blanchard, a white, racist college boy. 30 years later, her son tracks down the now wealthy magnate for revenge.

Yeager's found his play. He shifts into high gear. "We film the truth. First, what actually went down, the brutality, the rape. On stage, Blanchard's lies, she was a whore, he bought her, she gave him what he paid for."

Casting from his ensemble, Yeager hits a wall, finding a black actress to play Willow. No Willow, no play.

Dejected for days, then, a break. The actor playing Willow's son, Les Irons, tells us about a young singer working at Radiant, a downtown club.

Uneasy going inner-city, we ask Les to drive us. The club is RADIANT! Black mirrored front, thick glass doors. A valet opens the car door, we get out, he parks it.

A high energy crowd, all black, lines up in front of Radiant. Guys, high end casual, ladies, designer chic. Me and Yeager, jeans, tees, and sneakers. Nobody gives us a second glance. Les walks us to the head of the line, nods to the door man. He unhooks the velvet rope and waves us in. A smiling host leads us to front seats. We order Cokes, and don't say a word. Everybody knows everybody, chatting table to table…a family.

The MC steps onstage. "You all came for one tiny, little thing."

The room shakes with applause, cheers, and whistles.

"And I won't keep you from her. Ladies and gentlemen," he pauses.

"Shilly Armstrong!"

The room goes black. A follow spot cuts through the darkness. A striking, sassy, self-assured young woman in a black sequined dress strikes a pose in the hot white circle. Her adoring crowd gives Shilly a standing ovation.

A sharp nod to the quartet, a trumpet growls, Shilly pulls the mic off the stand, and slides into Billie Holiday's "Easy Living."

Magnificent. I'm praying, 'Oh god, please, please, please.'

Shilly finishes her set. Deafening applause, again. She curtsies gracefully and glides down the stage steps. A waiter gives her a flute of Champagne.

Shilly raises the glass toward her fans. "To ya'll, my little darlins."

All toast back, more adulation, she bows for a moment, then starts backstage. Les rushes up, whispers a few words. She laughs out loud. All eyes on her, she speaks so all can hear, peering right at me and Yeager, "I'm no actress, I play me, only me."

Now the room is silent. The spot should be on us, sweating. Les hands Shilly a script. She takes it, maintaining eye contact, doesn't even glance, merely tosses it the bar trash can, and disappears backstage.

Again. Square one, no Willow, no play, but the muse of the theater is full of surprises.

Two weeks later, we're ready to pull the plug. Les rushes in. He points to the theater doors, they swing open and there she is, Shilly Armstrong in jeans, tee shirt, and sneakers, script in hand. "I read it. I like it. I'll do it."

Steve starts to talk.

Shilly abruptly cuts him off. "With conditions, non-negotiable," she rifles them off, "Daily ads in downtown papers, blankets downtown Baltimore with posters saying… Willow, A BLACK WOMEN'S REVENGE! Oh, and I almost forgot, 50% off for Black folks…period. Call me when we start rehearsals." She spins and disappears through the doors.

Steve and I are whiter than the white we are. But we got WILLOW, with conditions. And can she act. Instinctively. She proves that on the film shoot.

"OK. First, we film the truth."

Steve takes over, his usual self. We scout locations. Shooting is fraught with emotion, three whites attacking a poor black woman, one raping her, but Shilly's cool, calm, and collected. She and I develop a working relationship of trust and respect. Her ideas, apt and welcome. We get what we came for, footage that makes the point without exploitation. My job, edit it. Steve's job, stage it.

On stage, Shilly's professional and opinionated. Steve respectfully takes her feedback while never compromising his vision. They do it together, creating a unique, real-life character. Film and stage melded telling the story Rashomon style. Reviews are solid. "Willow" is extended a full month. Unknown to anyone, a New York talent scout agent from William Morris Agency was in the audience. After the performance he slipped backstage to Shilly's dressing room. He raves about how talented she is. Offers to represent her. She signs on the dotted line. He'll keep in touch if anything that suite her comes up. She's thrilled. Never tells anyone. Shilly's secret.

The cast party is a jubilant and joyous affair. Around 1:00 am, Shilly says she's exhausted, needs to cab home.

Steve jumps right in. "I'll drive ya. It's on my way."

Shilly spins, faces me. "How about you drive, Mick? You don't have a date, Steve's got two." So, off we go.

Her place, a loft, eclectic, cool, comfortable. She collapses onto her overstuffed black leather sofa, kicking off her shoes.

"Before you park, there's a bottle of bubbly in the fridge, two glasses in the freezer."

Surprised, I get the bottle and glasses, and POP! We toast "Willow" and "Shilly Takes Manhattan." We for hours. She takes a pee break, I check my watch, whoa, four-thirty.

I stand up as she floats back in, barefoot. "I should get back."

"Back to who?" Shilly asks. Good point.

"Well, I am the party host."

She chirps, "Everybody's crashed or gone."

"Okay, one quick night cap to our future," I say as she hands me my glass. Cling! Sip. Saunter.

I open the door.

"See ya tomorrow?" she purrs.

"Well, no. Filming's finished. My part's done."

Shilly, sincerely surprised, "Then this is it, goodbye?"

"I'll drop by the theater once in a while to keep in touch," I jabber.

"I hope so. It was a treat meeting and working with you, Mick. You are a classy guy. I'll miss you." Shilly leans in, kisses me on the cheek. "Till whenever," she smiles.

I walk out. She slowly closes the door.

The elevator beckons, but I can't move. I'm frozen. Mind whirling. Shilly's door opens.

"I saw you through the peep hole. Anything wrong?," she asks.

"No, I…I…" In a flourish, Shilly engulfs me, we kiss, no cheek this time,

pulls me inside, shuts the door with a flick of her bare foot.

We stay together. A cultural whirlwind. Black night life, meeting her family, cooking Shilly's mama my crab cakes, feasting on her Jambalaya. They literally adopt me. I never felt more welcome, accepted. Something my white family could never do.

One night making love, I sense she's elsewhere. Not in our zone.

"Anything wrong, baby. You seemed a little…" She puts a finger to my lips shushing me. I see tears forming in her eyes. "I…I kept a secret from you. I had no idea we were going to…to…"

"Just tell me Baby. It can't be anything we can't work through. Our love is too strong, just lay it out."

"Last year. Opening night. A William Morris agent can onto my dressing room. He loved my performance. Told me I have a future. Wanted to sign me, be my agent."

Me, "In New York City?"

"Yeah honey. I was overwhelmed."

"You signed?"

She breaks out. Full crying jag. "Yes. I signed. He said he'd call me. I didn't think anything would come of it."

"Well, your decision's been made. This is your break. You're an actress. I am thrilled and killed at the same time. I thought we could go on forever."

I pull her to me. Hug her naked shoulders maybe for the last time. I understand. I have my dreams too.

"I know, Mickey, Hollywood for you. New York for me. But maybe…"

"Yep. Maybe. No maybe for you, kid. Happen right now. I'll come up whenever I can. See if we can make it work out."

"Oh, Mickey. You're the best thing that's ever happened to me.."

"No. The best thing happened when you signed your name on that dotted line. Then the phone call. My darling, you are on your way."

I drive Shilly to Penn Station, Baltimore. "Come with me now," she chirps a loving plea.

"I can't go now."

"The draft?"

"Yeah. Two more years. Then…then, we'll see. Play it as it lays."

"Promise. Promise me you'll come to me every second you can."

"Of course, I will my darling girl. You are the center of my life. I love you."

She rushes into my arms. Just like in the movies that I dream to make one day in Hollywood. We smother with kisses. More tears. Both.

The PA announces her train. Our hands clasped, Shilly starts down the steps to the platform. Slow motion. Hands slip apart. She blows kisses. Shilly looks up at me. Mouths words. I don't have to hear them. I feel them. More air kisses as she enters the coach. Sliding door close on this extraordinary woman. Not mine anymore. I know it. Maybe I knew it all along.

The train rolls away, taking Shilly to her future. Her dream come true. I know my turn will come. I'll make it happen.

We try to make it work. Long distance love affairs have a short life. Star-crossed from the start. She falls for a rising Sax player. We try friendship. You know how that is. Me? Alone…again.

European Customs

My fourth year of teaching. Jr. High school science. Got a high number in the national Vietnam draft lottery. A free man!

I spot Annie Preston at our first teachers' meeting. New art teacher, not really my type, too much black eye make-up, but definitely arousing. Upscale hippie look. Mismatched clothes, way high-end rags. Black stiletto heels…in conservative Maryland middle school…oh my.

Pass Annie's room every morning. Touch of flirting going on. Makes me feel good. I'm available after the painful end of a long-term relationship. Annie stops, "I'm having a small get to know you party Saturday. Join us?"

Mental flash, are you kidding, "Absolutely. What's your pleasure."

"Awfully personal aren't you."

"Meant what's your drink of choice?"

Black lined eyes flashing, "I know. Just teasing. Red wine, beer, vodka, your call. 8:00 Directions, in your mailbox."

"Thanks for thinking of me, Annie."

"Been doing a lot of that lately."

Whoa. Talk about personal. Dig it. Anxious.

The party is indeed small. Six teachers. Cream of the crop. Two couples, me and Annie. Surprise, surprise. The weed comes out. Careful. We're the example setters, but—not tonight. We get tipsy and high. Dance to The Stones, toke to The Doors. Two a.m., the party breaks up. Couples leave. Me and Annie, alone.

"Guess I better shove off."

"Tomorrow's Saturday, Mickey, Our day off, Mickey! Stay a bit?"

Mind-speak, I can stay forever, if I should be so lucky. And I am. She hands me a fresh glass of Cabernet. Leans in too close to ignore. We kiss. I set down my glass, pull her on my lap. Much later, Mick and Annie, friends with benefits. Maybe a couple. See each other a lot. Her place or mine. One sweet eve in bed, post coital glow, Annie says, "What are you doing this summer?"

"No plans. Went to Europe last year. Good and bad."

"Up for another trip? Erase the bad, I'm going to Paris for a month?"

"Alone?"

"Not if you come with."

Well, well, well. Start packing Mick.

Paris with a cool woman on your arm is way different then last time. Magical, a cliché. *Une ville d'amour*, for sure. She sparkles. I shine. Bistros every night. Wine, fab food. Benefits at night. Could not be better. Two weeks of bliss.

One morning I wake and Annie's not there, her suitcase sits at the end of bed. Closed. What the hell? I dress, go down for our morning continental breakfast. Annie's not there. She comes back later. Serious.

"Mick."

Not Mickey. Not good.

"We should talk."

Me thinkin' downhill. Come on. It can't be…It is.

Annie, "It's not that I don't like you a lot, but…"

Prep for a spoken Dear John. Heart drops to stomach.

Annie, "I'm going to fly back earlier."

"May I ask why?"

"Unfinished business. I just popped up."

"How early is your flight?"

"Three this afternoon. I had a wonderful time." Cheek to cheek kiss.

"Me as well," I said.

Annie, "I going to that little curio we found. Get some gifts. Then, the airport."

"You want me to…"

"No. You stay, Enjoy the week."

She lightly squeezes my hand. Walks away. Doesn't look back. Curtains. I head for the hotel bar. Only ten AM. Order a bloody Mary. Easier on a dropped guy's gut. Another Mary. Double shot. Go back to our…my room. Crash. Wake up. Check the clock. Four o'clock. She's gone. My *raison d'etre* bailed.

Paris alone. No more amour. I hit La Coupole. Spot a couple of British guys laughing over drinks One eyes me. Walks over.

"Name's Randolph, Randy. We shake firmly. "Traveling alone?"

"I am since this morning."

"We saw you with your lady. Very nice."

"While it lasted."

Randy, "Seduced and abandoned."

Me, "Right as rain."

Randy, "Been there, mate. Come join us for a drink, on me."

I go. Meet Jacob, Jake. Cool blokes. We bond. Fun to the max. Folies Bergère. Just like the movies. All we need is Lautrec. Takes my mind off my heart. The weekends. Randy and Jake are taking Ostend to Dover ferry in the morning. I have a week before my flight. Haven't done Britain.

"Mind if I go with ya."

"Not at all. Mate. Not at all. We can share a room. Go in style. And…the boat has a bar."

Train to Ostend. Board the ferry. Bunks nice. Head for the bar. Drinks on the guys.

A few later, Randy, "Got a favor, Mick." Shows me a new camera, "My hobby's photography."

I smile, "So's mine. Develop and print my own stuff." Another bond.

Randy, "One of the reasons I came over was to pick this up. Too expensive at home. New government put in a stiff luxury tax."

Jake jumps in, "Fifty friggin' per cent."

Randy, "If you take the camera in, no tax."

Gullible me, "Sure, why not."

Randy, "Here's the receipt. Read it so you know the details."

I tuck it in my shirt pocket. They buy another round. Next morning, hangover. Head feels like a bass drum in a marching band. We debark. Move to customs. I stand in line in front of the guys. My turn. The customs guy looks hang dog. Way too serious. Checks my passport,

"American?" the customs guy asks.

"Yes sir."

"Purpose of your trip?"

"Vacation. Paris."

No reaction.

"Anything to declare?"

"I bought this camera."

His hand shoots out. No words. I take it from around my neck. Hand it over. He looks at it, turning it in his hands. Looks at me.

"What kind of camera is it?" he asks.

Me, easy. I know it. "Thirty-five millimeter. Single reflex."

Official, "What make?"

Oh. God. The receipt. Never checked. Bluff, "Un oh, "I... I forgot."

Him, "Forgot? How much was it?"

I'm lost. I guess. "Couple of hundred."

"American money?"

106

"Travelers checks."

Him, "You have a receipt?"

"Yes, sir." Fish it out of my pocket. He snatches it.

"Says here, 350 quid. British pounds. Name of shop you bought it?"

No idea. Brit pals put some distance between us in the line. Cold sweat starts, "I'm not sure."

"Traveling alone?" Turn to my pals. Randy turns his back. Not good.

Official, hawk eyed, "Those two men. Do you know them?"

Dead in the water. No more lies. "Yes. Sir."

Official gestures to the guys, commands, "Would you two step up please."

Randy and Jake walk up, grim faced.

Official, "I see you have two cameras round your neck. Photographers?"

Randy, "Yes, sir. Bought them here years ago."

Official, hand out. Randy passes them over along with an old crumpled receipt. "Pro-Photo. 35 Langley. Liverpool. Where I live from. Cost me 50 quid in 1968."

Official, "Do you know what I think? I think you conned this Yank to bring this new camera in for you, avoid the tax."

Smugglers. Caught.

Official. "Give me the absolute truth, now, for your own good."

Randy, "Yes, sir."

Official, points to Randy and Jake, "You two, step over here." He gestures. Two other nearby officials walk over.

First official, "Clemens, escort these two into room four. Dodson, take the American to room six."

They go one way, me another. I'm escorted, put in a room with a ratty folding table, one folding chair.

Dodson, "Hands against the wall, legs spread."

Deep nausea, I do as he says. He frisks me. Rough.

"Disrobe."

"Pardon?"

"Remove your clothing."

"Can I keep my...?"

"All means all. Now."

Cold sweat pouring. A strip search. Frightening. Humiliating.

Nude against the wall. Dodson, snaps on rubber gloves. Takes out small flashlight...torch. Spreads my ass cheeks...wide.

"Turn please."

I pivot. Shaking. He lifts my scutum. Aims torch.

"You can dress now. Sit in the chair." He leaves.

I wait for at least an hour. Head racked. More sweat. Want to throw up. Keep it down.

The head official from the line comes in. He reads my name from my passport. "Alexander Benderoth, you have broken the law."

I'm ready to piss my pants, maybe shit. My amorous trip turns into hell on earth.

Official, "Have you ever done this before?"

"No sir."

"Why now?"

Tearing up. It pours out. "I met these guys. We hung out. They asked a favor. I had no idea..."

"You'd get caught."

"Yes sir."

"You know how serious smuggling is?"

Tears roll down my cheek. "Yes sir."

"Sit. I will be back shortly."

Shortly becomes two hours. He returns stone-faced. "I have called your embassy and explained the situation. They have no legal authority in this matter. I'm very sorry, but You will be detained..."

The rest is in slow, slow motion, his words sound slurred.

"…for five days in The Bristol lock up. Plus, a fine of 300 us dollars. Payable immediately."

Two other customs officers return. Dodson handcuffs me. Handcuffs. Cold. Hurt. I pay the cashier. All my checks. Then I'm prodded to the Paddy wagon with several other shady looking chaps, including my partners in crime. We do not speak.

Bristol lockup. Stripped again. Showered. Green baggy jumpsuit. The long walk. Cell bars. Night stick xylophone. Not music. The guard stops, waves his arm. Cell door slides open automatically. Bunks on either side. Right side, top, bottom taken by my roomies. Bottom asleep.

Top bunk pal, "Take the top, mate. Bit of a climb, no blokes over ya."

I comply. Still overhung. Toss up my pillow and binky.

Top holds out hand. We shake, "Matthew R. Darwell, call me R. You?"

"Mick Benderoth. Mick's fine."

R, "Mick? Irish?"

"Half."

"Good enough. Me hundred proof. In for?"

Why beat around the bush, "Smuggling?"

"Drugs?"

"Camera."

"Luxury mule, eh." I nod climbing to my bunk. Need to rest my flummoxed head. R's a talker. Nonstop. Good point. I don't have to answer. Whistle screech!

R, "Chow, mate." Our cell door slides open. R steps out. I follow his every move. Veteran teacher. Sleeper out cold.

Mess hall. Just like the movies…again. Me, eyed by the murmuring diners. Follow R to the line. Stained metal tray, three wells. Plop! Some brown stew something. Plot! Mashed spuds. Plop! Cabbage cooked during the famine. Aroma. Gaggous. Two thin, stale bread slices. Bottled water. Bread and water. Jail food. I sit, try the brown ooze. Gristled gristle. Cabbage, slurm. Spuds, powered.

R, smiling mixes it all together, "Better this way, mate, can't tell what yer eating, but eat up, nothin' till morning."

Hold my breath, I force it down. Swallow

Middle of night I bolt up, gurgling, nauseous, don't make it to the W.C. Barf all over myself and bed. Thank god no one sleeping beneath. Food poisoning. Fill the bowl twice.

R, "Least ya didn't shite in yer duds. No clean ones till shower time."

Bed ridden. Do my time vertically. Released, showered, my own duds. On some Bristol street to nowhere. Penniless. R slips me a fiver as he hops the bus.

"R, you don't have to," I say, accepting the fiver.

R, "Don't have but I want to. Irish blood runs deep. Don't play the sucker next time, Pub round the corner. Pint first, then eat. They'll steer ya to a B & B. Take good care, lad."

We shake, my only friend in four thousand miles pulls away. Bangers and mash at the pub. Two pints of bitter. B & B down the street. Spare. Only for one night.

I take the bus to the airport. Dig my balled-up ticket from my nap sack. Scan the board. Flight in twenty. Head for the bar. Holy fucking shit. Annie and some guy, arm in arm stroll in. We lock eyes. She flushes. Pulls guy up to me.

"Mickey. Mickey," she says.

Mind-speak. Yeah, Mickey, you b...b... b...bite tongue...Mickey.

Annie, "What a surprise. Guess you're wondering..."

I eye the guy. "No. I read the tea leaves."

Annie, "What? Oh well. Meet Roger. Long story short..."

"Don't need to hear it." I turn my back. Sit at the bar. "Guinness, please."

Flash forward. Twenty years. Now married. My wife Nancy has two teenage daughters. Nancy is away on a location scout for a new commercial she's producing for our company.

Becky is at college. Sarah, the youngest, is prepping for her first trip to Europe. Taking a red eye.

Night before she departs, I take her aside, ask, "You carrying?" She looks at me with her sweet, bright baby blues, "You're kidding. After that story you keep telling us."

Sarah is busted with joints in her cutesy white, turned down ankle socks. Strip searched, detained, fined. Will we ever learn? Not me. Not her. Not nobody.

European customs.

Hunt

We frequent Mackey's, a local bar across the tracks in Reading PA, 'cause Mackey doesn't card. A well-worn hangout for locals attached to the bottle. Space aged. Four card tables and Mackey's one prize. His pockmarked metal bar, rimmed in ancient oak.

Two frat brothers, Brad Clampet, and Phil Roth, both from Pennsylvania farm families, and me, a Baltimore City kid, dive into Mackey's to discuss weekend plans.

Sipping his beer, Brad says he's going home. "First day of deer season, family tradition's a hunt."

Guns, killing animals, macho bullshit, not on my playlist.

Phil asks if he can join. Brad nods yes, turning to me, "Why don't you come, Mick?."

"Thanks, but no thanks," I murmur sipping my Scotch.

Phil chuckles, "I know, city boy, hunting's for red necks."

"Your words, not mine," I counter.

"Stereotypes man, you're beyond that, come with us, broaden your horizons," Phil jests, mocking my current new age catch phrase.

Brad earnestly replies, "Hunting puts food on our tables."

"And a rack on the wall," I grimace. They persist. Feeling the Scotch, I reticently give in.

It's a two-hour drive to Brad's house. Large white, palatial. His two older brothers, mother, and father, welcomed us warmly. Definitely not red necks. Brad's father is a surgeon, his mother a college professor. Brothers in med school. Dinner, congenial. Long day. Crash early.

Next afternoon, Brad ushers me to the garage. On the wall, a mahogany glass front gun closet with a massive padlock. Just the sight of all those rifles makes me cringe. He opens it, browses for a time, then takes one from the center.

"Aged, well cared for, fierce looking Remington 3030 replete with Bausch & Lomb scope," Brad says admiringly. "First gun I bought myself."

He proudly hands it to me.

I freeze.

"Just hold it. It's not loaded."

I forbiddingly reach out and grasp the neck of the weapon. Just the weight wrenched my stomach. The smell of gun oil sifts into my nostrils. Not a friendly odor.

"Now pay attention." Brad patiently shows me how to handle and use the bolt to inject a fierce looking cartridge into the breach.

A lifetime first. Holding a loaded gun. He senses my unease.

"Cool down. The lock's on." After lunch we'll go to the range, sight in the scope, practice aiming and firing.'

I am not looking forward to it. The range, packed. Men, boys, young, old, a few women, target shooting. They make guns look like part of their bodies. A booth opens.

"You're up, Mick," Brad orders.

Cautiously I raise the rifle to my shoulder, squint through the scope and fire. The recoil slams the scope into my eye, black for weeks. The butt spins me off balance, nearly knocking me over. Firepower. Horrifyingly exhilarating.

"Let's get some ice for that eye. My fault, should have warned you." Thanks, fearless leader.

After dinner that night, Brad walks me to a coat closet, takes out the ubiquitous red and black wool plaid coat, offers it to me.

116

"Fleece lined, gonna be cold." Pinning a clear plastic hunting license on the back, he says, "Now you're official."

Legal deer killer, my bowels twitch.

Brad adds, "Insulated gloves and a wool lined hat in the pockets. Wear two pair of socks."

After a night cap, we hit the sack. The next morning, Brad shakes me from a deep sleep. I start, not realizing where I am. It sinks in. The hunt. It's still pitch-black outside. I get dressed in my hunting garb.

Brad says, "Time to meet the party, Hoover's Diner."

We pull up, rush inside, escaping the freeze. A cliché kind of place, popular with the locals, complete with gum-chewing waitresses. Stool-seated hunters, roughhewn bunch of rugged men stare into steaming black coffee in their cups. Brad, and his father, warmly greeted by all. Frat bro. Phil knows some of the men. My intro, cooler, handshakes, nods, grunts, a few smiles.

Whispered aside to Brad, "Not the most cordial welcome."

He nudges me over to a cigarette machine, buys a pack of Lucky's. Two pack a day man, replete with cough. He rips off the cellophane, taps one out, puts it between his lips, snaps a lighter, takes a drag, smoke flowing from his mouth up his nostrils.

"Always wary of a new guy," he whispers. "Feel it's bad luck."

Great. I'm an omen.

"Forget it. It's my hunt, I call the shots." He smiles, smoke billowing.

Breakfast over, we drive the highway for miles, turn off, pulling up to a formidable red pipe gate. No trespassing sign dangling. One man jumps out of his pickup, unlocks the padlock, swings it open, waves the hunters in, relocks the gate.

A dirt road, dense forest line both sides. Pickups kick up dust clouds. Headlight beams barely cut through. No matter.

They know this road by heart. The caravan reaches an open plot, vehicles pull in, park, we all pile out. In the dawn light, Brad takes control, spreads a weathered map on his truck hood. "First pass, Asher, Wilkes, Brennen, Todd, beaters, guys who chase game through the dense woods in hunter's range. Stand twenty meters apart," pointing at the map, "Here, here, here, and here. Phil, Mick and me, shooters, here, here, and here. I'll place them. Rest of you know the lay. Let's do it."

Silently the men disappear into the woods as the sun fully breaks the horizon.

Brad faces Phil and me, says, "Hand gestures from now on. Follow me."

We walk for twenty minutes, finally stopping at a small path.

Brad leans into Phil, "Fifty feet in, a clearing facing a corn field, beaters driving through it."

Phil nods and walks away. Brad and I continue walking. Another fifteen minutes, grade raising sharply, me out of breath, we stop at the crest of a high hill overlooking a field boarded by woods on three sides.

Brad faces me grinning, "You get the prime spot." He points right, "Beaters drive to that side. Any deer will break right there. There's goddamn party stalking the woods. Found out at Hoover's. Fuckers shouldn't be there. Out-of-staters. Nothing like rivals to boost a greenback's spirits. I'm going to hike to my spot. Make me proud, Mickey."

No pressure here. A slap on my back, he jogs away. Me, face frozen, at the top of a hill, staring at an empty field.

Half hour later a breeze picks up. Wind chill burns my cheeks. So far nothing. Another twenty minutes, frozen solid, I see something materialize out of the woods. A deer? Oh, yeah. A big buck with a trophy rack. Hartford Insurance commercial. Mouth dry, I raise the scope to my sore eye, cross hairs at his flank. Finger on trigger. Epiphany. I snap out of a primal haze. What the hell am I doing? This is not me. I will not do this. I raise the barrel skyward and fire. The stag takes off into the left field. Within seconds, *Blam!, Blam!, Blam!* Three shots echo. The other party. I drove my prize right to them. Self-fulfilling prophecy, bad luck.

Brad races up. "I saw it. A hundred yards away. What happened?"

Lying, "I...I missed. I heard shots."

Friggin' other party. Forget it, you get another chance next year, Let's move further up the hill. I wanna see these assholes."

Fifteen minutes up the rocky dirt road, weathered farm silos in the distance. We come to a small clearing. Five men and a teenage boy, stand over the fallen prey. Brad's pissed. Really pissed. He watches silently as one man, coat on the ground beside him, field dresses the buck. Revolting. Nauseated. He pulls a metal cup from his coat pocket, scoops it into the deer's open gut, filling it with blood. He turns victoriously, thrusts the cup to the boy. The boy takes it proudly, drinks deep. The men cheer.

Brad hisses, "That was your stag, you should be drinking."

Shocked at what I'm seeking and his vehemence, I have no words. He slumps back down the road. First and last new horizon for me. Never broach it with Brad, never touch a gun again.

Jimi Jam

Night on the town. NYC, 1967, still the Big Apple, a fantastical realm to us southern boys. My brother Steve's first rock album, "Graffiti" was released by ABC records today, a hybrid of West Coast psychedelic, CSN harmonies, blues, rock, jazz, classical artful mélange, spectacular. Never realized Steve's childhood head hums could coalesce into this masterpiece, way ahead of its time. Advance rave reviews. Big time. Party time. The world's Steve's oyster, sadly, sans pearl…but that's another story.

Tonight, we take the town. Steve's college roomie, Bob, an up-and-coming copywriter at a high-end ad agency gets underground grapevine skivvy, Jimi Hendrix first album "Are You Experienced," Jimi's guitar licks way, way outta the box. released today. Today? Coincidence, I don't think so, but maybe. Serendipity squared, maybe. I mean, my bro, Steve, and Jimi Hendrix debut albums, same day. I'm flipping out.

Jimi's album will break the mold for rock guitarists. Jimi Hendrix, true original, one of a kind, electric guitar genius. Period. Graffiti? That's another story. Some other time.

Jimi's is showcasing "Are You Experienced" at a tiny village club, The Cellar. Sold out before it was sold out. Bobbo finagles tickets.

Serendipity number two, Eddie Kramer, world renowned British recording engineer; Woodstock, Joni, CSN, THE BEATLES!, doing sound for Jimi's gig. Kramer engineered

Steve's "Graffiti" and Hendrix's "Are You Experienced."
Same studio. Side by side. Beyond serendipity.

So here we are. Stage front waiting for Jimi. Nice surprise.
Eddie Kramer taps Steve on the shoulder.

"Hey, Stevie, surprised ta see ya, chap. Congrats on the
vinyl." Eddie pats his hand. "Ya did good, lad. You and Jimi
same day. Pretty fuckin marvi if I say so me-self. C'mon
backstage after his set, get acquainted." Gestures fingers to lips,
"Have a toke." Winks. Devilish. "Later chappies."

What? What? What? Is this really happening? Steve smiles.
His element at last.

Kramer slips away and up the spiral staircase to the sound
booth.

Stage lights come up. Mitch Mitchel, Jimi's mega drummer
first on stage. Sits at his kit. Tweaks hit-hat, kick drum thump,
thump! Noel Redding, coveted electric bass player, out next.
Plugs into a Marshall amp, taller than me on his shoulder. The
patch cord buzz alone is deafening.

Stage goes black a beat. Crowd nervously quiet. A louder
patch cord rasp cut through the silence *Screeeonk!!!* Light up full.
Jimi Hendrix, in eclectic Hendrix fashion, replete with
signature red head band, wry grin then Kaboom! The room
explodes with a sound like no other. Jimi blitzin' out "Purple
Haze." Unreal! He plays every cut on the album. Sounds a
guitar never meant to make, made, more, more, and more.

Crowd on our feet, screaming cheers. Jimi Hendrix hands
his ax to his tech, lights up a Marlboro, slides-glides off stage.
Followed by Mitch and Noel. Don't get no more musicalicious
than this. Ever. Then it does.

Kramer and Hendrix pull chairs up to our table. Waitress
appears, bottle of Commemorativa Tequila, best there is,
fixin's, limes and salt. Before we get a chance to praise his set,
Jimi holds out his hand to Steve. They shake.

"Steve, right?" Jimi asks.

Steve, wordless, nods.

"I'm Jimi."

So cool, so demure. "Eddie digs your sound. Played me "Jingle Jangle Woman." Outta sight, Stevie."

Stevie! First name basis with Jimi.

"Thanks…Jimi," Steve says.

Jimi nods to me.

I struggle to remember my name, "Mick…Steve's brother."

We shake. I'll never wash it. We all chat, smoke killer Oaxacan, Tequila shots.

Jimi hands me a roach. "You in 'Graffiti,' Mick?"

"I wish."

Steve sweetly, "But he played drums with our bands since we were ten."

"Skins, huh. "Good?"

Steve, "Yes, he is."

"So, Stevie. You're 'Graffiti's' aces bass man. You wrote the album."

"Yes."

"Super chops. I heard ya turned way up." Jimi, a shot, a puff. "Know what? Noel and Mitch are with some chicks, fueling for the next set. You guys wanna jam?"

What'd he say? Am I hearing right? JAM! YES, YES, and again YES!

Jimi, quick toke, "Let's do it."

He jumps on stage, Steve behind him. I can barely walk. Emotional overload!!! Playing drums with Jimi Hendrix. I died. In heaven. I take Mitch's throne. Gingerly pick up sticks from his leather pouch hanging on a kick drum lug.

Jimi, nods to Steve, "Blues groove in E." Nods to me. I count off. Wham! We're inside Jimi's groove. His blues licks astral. Solos uncanny. We cook. Play for eternity. It seems. Finale crescendo reshapes my cosmos. We end. Feel like I ran a marathon. Me and Steve dripping sweat. Jimi, nary a drop.

Standing ovation. Mitch and Noel meander on stage, back slaps for us all.

Noel takes his bass from Steve, "Still warm, mate. Made er' scream."

Pats his bass. "I call her Marylin, blond and beautiful."

They take their rightful spots, slam to their second set. Ethereal.

Jimi is a different species. He is his music. It just don't get more musicalicious than this. Jammin' with Jimi. I carry this eternal moment forever Momentarily immortal…sort of…but that's another story.

Songbird

Music is my passion. I write my own tunes, rocky blues. My stage name is Steve Preston. It scans better than Straussbourg. I built my recording studio in the basement room from scratch with top of line hard and software. I write, play, record, mix, stream…endlessly. No one wants my music. Two years, nothing.

I get a beer from the fridge. Check my email for anything remotely hopeful. Zilch. Politicians pleading for donations, endless ads for nothing. I delete, delete, delete. Stop. An odd one catches my eye. "Open me first," right out of Lewis Carrol. It reads, "Singing, my destiny. Got no songs. Desperate. My roommate Kira gave me your email address. Said you were a songwriter, she use'ta sing your songs in your band, "The Medulas." I sent you a song, "Broken Up," using Kira's hidden cell, before the attendants could find it."

No name, just an email address. Kira's roommate? Kira, Kira Langford. Long, long lost love. My old band's singer. Damaged beyond repair. Detox after detox. Rehab after rehab. Then, psych ward. I lost track. Now this? What the hell?

I listen to her song, "Broken Up." Wow! Way, way better than anything I ever wrote. This girl's the real deal.

Send her an email. "Loved 'Broken Up.' I'd like to lay it down. Let's meet."

Weeks. Not a peep. Whoever those attendants were musta found her cell. Attendants? Whatever. Put it out of my mind, back to work, gotta pay the bills. I'm a sound engineer for hire.

Made a bit of a name mixing and mastering. Pull all-nighter on clients' way late tracks. Coffeed out, exhausted. Try to sleep on the studio couch. Head just hits the cushion. The doorbell blasts Hendrix's "Manic Depression." Meant to change it, something less manic. I bolt upstairs. Open the front door. Am I awake? Dreaming? A girl. About my age, tangled, knotted dirty blond hair, filthy hospital gown, bloody bare feet, staring deep into my eyes.

"It's me. The singer. Kira's friend."

"How's Kira doing?"

"Hung herself with a torn bed sheet."

Kira. Dead. Jesus.

"I need a bathroom. Now."

"It's right…" Before I can finish, she starts peeing on the floor, unmoving. I take her hand and rush her into the john as she makes a trail across the floor. Leaves the bathroom door open, lifts her gown sits and finishes. She floats out past me, like a sylph.

"I broke out. I'll stay here. They won't find me. I need to sleep. Now."

"Ah, use my…my bedroom. Down the hall."

Slow baby steps. Me, behind. She walks into the room, turns and faces me.

"No sex…just music." Crashes. Out cold.

I close the door and get a sponge to clean the floor. Freaked. My mind races. Broke out? Stay here? Get a beer from the fridge. Sit on the couch. Still groggy from last night. I'll deal with this in the morning. Chug beer. Turn out the light. Lay back…yeah, in the morning.

Music wakes me. From my studio. She's using my acoustic, singing "Broken up." I go downstairs. She pays me no attention. Finishes the song. Me, flummoxed.

Says deadpan, "Let's do it. Now."

Spellbound, I mic her and my guitar, sit at the board. She sings. Whoa momma! Am I hearing this? A natural. She owns it. Playback. Got it in one take.

"What's your name?"

Nonplus, "Pick one." Silently walks upstairs into the bedroom. Crashes, again.

What the hell have I gotten myself into?

Next morning. She's back in the studio. Listening. I make coffee. Two mugs. Go down. Hand her one.

"Coffee?"

"Makes you crazy."

Crazy? Crazier?

She finds an old dog eared, coffee ringed copy of Fleetwood Mac's *Rumors* on my coffee table. Points to a Christine McVie tune.

"That's my name."

I glance "Songbird?"

"Songbird"

"Ok, Songbird. We gotta talk."

Not listening, again, she says, "I have to change my look, so they won't know me. Drugstore, hair dye...blue...light blue. I'm going to take a bath."

I don't even question. Go to the drugstore. Buy hair dye. Counter girl recommends.

Walking home a flyer stapled to a utility pole catches my eye. A picture dead center. Holy crap!. It's her. Songbird. Ashley Carter. Escapee from Belford Sanitarium. If you see her call Dr. William Menderson. I write the phone number on the drugstore receipt, put it in my wallet.

Back to my place. Songbird, Ashley, whoever, is sitting on the closed toilet seat. Towel wrapped.

"Got the dye?." I hand her the box. "I'm hungry. Make me some food...anything." She kicks the door closed with a badly scratched foot.

I make tuna sandwiches. Her voice from behind startles. "Look at me." I turn. Eyes pop. Her hair, cut ultra-short, color, blue fade. "I used your beard trimmer."

Raided my closet. Wears my extra-large, ripped Kurt Cobain tee, it just covers her knees. I have no words. Instant icon. Singer Songbird is born. In the kitchen, Songbird gobbles the food like she hasn't eaten for, who knows? I keep the flyer phone number to myself.

After eating, Songbird blurts, "I need girl's clothes. I can't go buy. I might be seen. You go."

Me? I know nothing about girl's stuff. Then I remember, say, "My sister's in LA. Left a lot of stuff. Check out her closet."

Songbird emerges in a somber grey mock. Feet bare. Still the girl standing in my doorway. She naps. I grab a beer, plop on the couch. Forty winks Something wakes me. Songbird's voice from my studio again. Definitely not what I recorded.

Dash down. Songbird sits at the console. She's overdubbed her songs. Songbird knows how to engineer. Gob smacked. I have to tell someone about her. I call Rick Salter, my drummer, best friend. He comes by with Sandy, lead guitarist and Brandon bass guitar. My back up band since forever.

Songbird walks into the studio. Heads snap. Mouths drop.

"Guys, meet Songbird, singer, song writer."

She nods. Sits yoga style on the floor. I play her song. Not a word, not a sound, not a move, the guys frozen. It ends. Silence.

Songbird from her perch, "I have to sleep. Now." She disappears upstairs.

Sandy, "Whoa, whoa, whoa. Who is she?"

"Songbird."

"Songbird. Yeah, yeah. Songbird."

We practice with her for a week until she nods, "Yes."

Her moves, slow, vulnerable, hypnotic. Her spirit engulfs the studio. She nails every song. We call our new band, Songbird. What else?

I call in a favor. Frank Pierson, owner of Club Nuance. Pierson generously gives us a Saturday night spot, sight unseen, opening for Rivers End, an up and comer. Club Nuance, packed for Rivers End.

Pierson introduces us. To the chanting, "Rivers End, Rivers End."

Pierson, "Cool it. River's next." Crowd boos, hisses. "But first, we welcome a new band Songbird. Audience claps lackadaisically. Songbird steps to the mike still wearing my sister's grey smock, still barefoot. Caresses it. She sways, sashays through the musical intro of her song, "Broken Up." The audience intrigued, quiets. Not a murmur. *Songbird's* voice blasts off. The crowd runs stage front, all eyes on this, this, Songbird. They know they are witnessing something way new, unique. Songbird weaves her spell. My heart swells.

Then I notice Songbird's mood changing. She gets more and more aggressive. The band guys shrug nervously eyeballing each other.

Then, a manic explosion as she screams, "Fuck you mother fuckers. Aimless fucking sheep. Stupid. You should bow to me. You are mine. I'll will lead you."

The audience frozen.

Her rant intensifies, "Bunch of mindless asshole cocksuckers!" She spits at them, arms flailing, throws the mike stand into the crowd. A girl is hit, goes down. I run up and try to pin her arms. Faces me. A crazed beast. Scratches my face.

Pierson nods to the bouncers. They take the stage. She fights with inhuman strength. Suddenly she collapses to the floor, quivering convulsively. EMT's show up, strap Songbird onto the gurney, wheeled into ambulance. Squeals away, siren blaring. Tears and blood stream down my face. I'm in shock. I pull the phone number from my wallet. Make the call.

I meet Dr. Menderson in the ER. He reads me the riot act.

Head bowed, I say nothing. All my fault. Nauseous. Guilt ridden. Kira. Now Songbird?

Nightmares rake my dreams. I must see her.

I call and go to the Sanitarium. Menderson kindly leads me to her room. She's strapped down. Does not recognize me. Lives in the songbird world locked forever in her head.

A month. Two. Play her album obsessively. I call to set up another visit. Menderson's deep baritone "I'm sad to say Ashley is dead. Complications from electro-therapy."

Kira, now Ashley, dead. I drop to the couch. Vomit bitter bile. Recluse for days.

I slowly recover. Compulsively spread Songbird's "Broken Up" over the internet, dedicated to Ashley and Kira. Quickly noticed. Notoriety didn't hurt. Picked up by a major label. Streamed everywhere. National hit.

Songbird's single goes platinum. A tribute to lost souls, dying to sing.

Spider Guy

Nineteen sixty-five. A long, serious relationship with Lesley, my woman, destined to marry, ends with betrayal.

I'm a Baltimore filmmaker with dreams of Hollywood, I thought Lesley would be by my side. Life threw me a curve. Trying to rebound. I am deeply pained. Feel so alone.

Job to avoid Vietnam draft. Teach Junior High School. Passion, filmmaking. Dream. Hollywood. I'm making a film for a multi-media play, with partner Steve Yeager. Work keeps me from unraveling.

Rehearsal. Lunch break. The cast scatters. Steve, ever hustling, points out two girls in paint splashed overalls, painting the theater flat black.

Steve, smirking, "Our "cute little interns. Let's go get to know them."

We amble over to the Towson State College girls.

Steve grins deeper. "Looks like you're painting yourselves ladies. Are we working you too hard?"

The short, petite, brunette, sassily, "Got to get it up to our director's standards, isn't that so, Mr. Yeager and Mr. Benderoth."

Me, "Mick, just Mick. You guys?"

Tall, "I'm Angie Phillips."

Petite, "Krista…Krista Felloni, just Kris." We shake.

"Going into professional wall painting?" Steve jests.

Krista, sassy, "Towson State College. Drama. I wanted a low paying job with no future."

137

I laugh out loud. She's adorable. Sparks? Later, Steve is dating Angie, suggests a double with the four of us. I ponder. Am I ready?

Steve, "Come on man. Snap out of it. Get out there. Nothing to lose."

I go, surprise myself, have fun. First time in a while. Krista's smart, sensitive, charming. Spunky with a cool sense of humor, Sally Fieldish. Flying nun. Couple more dates, smitten. Make out at my apartment. Petting. Above the waist. Krista stops the hand I slip under her skirt. Boundaries. Made to be broken.

I meet Krista's adorable mother, Maria. Widowed fifteen years. Raised Krista alone. Devout Catholics. Loves to cook. Authentic Italian. Me, devout foodie. Maria offers a generous invite to their traditional family after Mass dinner. I pass on mass.

Maria serves Linguini Bolognese, baby dandelion greens, picked from her lawn that morning. A new delicacy. Scrumptious.

I also meet Krista's brother Mark, a prosperous florist, his wife Emma, a court stenographer and their three irrepressible kids. After eating, we all play dodgeball in the yard. Very cool family.

The following weekend, I take Krista and Maria out to dinner and a concert, Baltimore Symphony. Drop Maria off, take Kris back to my place. We make out. Aroused. Reclining on the couch.

"Want to move into the bedroom?" I ask.

"Mick, I've never done anything before." Krista, a virgin at nineteen? Surprised. "There's always a first time. You can spend the night?"

"No. It's not right." Not right?

I whisper, "We can go slow." She pulls away. Sits up.

"My mom's expecting me home." A definite hurdle. Petting. Period. Unsettling.

We keep seeing each other, love making on hold. Give it time. How much? I want to make love to her. I'm perplexed. What's next?

One night I take a flyer, "I think you should move in with me."

She's silent, then, "I…I don't know, Michalos," her nickname for me.

"Give us a chance to get to—"

Cuts me off, ardently. "My mom's very traditional. I'm all she has. She'd be alone." Maria's apparently her only confidant.

"Can you talk to her about it?"

She does. Maria's definitely not on board…at all.

Next time we're together, Krista says, "Wait!"

What? Wait? Again? I'm beginning to get a sad feeling. Catholic. Inexperienced. Emotionally tied to her mom. I think I love her.

"Michalos, I know I'm in love with you, but I can't. I'm sorry…please stop trying to convince me." Krista tries to steer me away from the subject.

I have to know if this is possible. I continue to broach. Do we have a future? Where the hell do I go from here? I'm frustrated. Desperate.

"Maybe we should stop seeing each other," I suggest.

"Is that what you want?"

"I don't know where we're going."

"I know. I know. It's so complicated."

Words tumble out, surprise me, "Let's get married." Jesus, did I just propose? Am I crazy? Maybe, but I love her. Do I? Enough? Marriage?

Krista's taken aback. I'm taken aback. She breaks into tears and hugs me. "Oh, Michalos. I…I'd want so much to say yes."

"Maybe you should run it by your mom. Get her feelings about it. Can you do that…for me? I just want us to be together."

A soft kiss, "Yes, I will."

Next night. Ebullient. "Mom loves you, loves us. Nothing would make her happier. Yes, Michalos, I'll marry you."

Am I Impetuous? Overreacting to—to what? My past? Best friends are shocked. Concerned. 'She's so young,' they all say. Is this the right thing for me? My ambition? Think hard Mick. No. No doubt. I want this. I want Krista. I'll marry her. That's that.

My mother is also ecstatic. Bonded with Krista from the get-go. She dives in. She and Maria are a joyous team. My father offers to pay for the wedding. Kris's brother steps up. They'll split it. My God. It's happening. A whirlwind. Me spinning, spinning. Out of control?

Her brother's friends, wedding planners. Date set. Elaborate gala in motion. No stopping now.

Wedding day. Krista ravishing in her sleek, mid-knee white dress at the altar. I've never seen an altar in my life. Weird.

Minister, Father Joe Conklin, the family priest, "Do you Mick Benderoth take…"

Deep breath. Mickey boy, this is it. "I do."

Father Conklin, "Krista?"

"Me too…yes, yes, I do."

The crowd titters at her adorable reply. We kiss. Done deal. You're not single any more, Mickey. What does that mean? Learn as you go?

Our honeymoon, Cape Cod. Wedding night. I sense Krista is not comfortable. We try to have sex. Kris is very nervous, almost in tears. We make love, badly, before, during, after. Patience, Mick, patience. You care for her. Love her.

We hit the beach, village, and restaurants, all fun. Love making, not so much. Patience, Mick. Patience. I'm frustrated.

Honeymoon over, we return to our normal lives. Normal?

I teach. Krista attends college. Love making is still a problem. She's just not into it. It's nineteen seventy, after four years and a high number in the Vietnam War draft lottery draft, my life plan surfaces. I tell Krista. I want to move to New York City and break into film. If I can make it there…then Hollywood. She's freaked. Way unsure. Just starting her junior year. Leaving school? Her mother is not happy. I stand firm. We're not in mommy land anymore, Krista. She agrees. Without enthusiasm.

I go to New York, find a cheap apartment, and back to Baltimore. We rent a U-Haul, pack and go, into the unknown.

Krista immediately gets a job as a receptionist at an architectural firm. Me, not so easy. I make the rounds. No. No. And no. CV? Not impressed. The advice I receive, "Go home. You were a big fish in a small pond."

An old college friend, Bob Lessing, a commercial copy writer, passes a tip. There's an editing firm looking for an intern. Intern? Work for free?

Bob says, "Take it man. Gotta start paying dues sometime."

I know he's right. I interview and get the job at fifty bucks a week. Krista carries us.

A year passes, then two. Krista yearns to go back to school. We compromise. She'll go back to college. We'll visit weekends. It works for a time. But long-distance strains a marriage.

I screw up big time. Have a fling with the secretary. A one-nighter turns into two, three. I do not like the guy I'm becoming. Careless, self-involved, blinded by the trek to my bliss. Hollywood film director.

At work, I rise quickly to assistant editor, at two fifty a week. Meets my nut. I visit and call Krista, less and less.

Bam! My journey begins. I get a dream job editing a documentary on black activist Malcolm X. The studio is Warner Bros. I've made the big time.

Bang! Bang! A fatal visit. Krista finds another woman's panties in the clothes basket. I don't even try to blubber my way through. Caught, plain and simple. She's my wife. I betrayed her. I hate myself.

Krista breaks down. Flood of tears. "I have to leave." Quickly packs, out the door. Rage is not her style.

What do I do? What can I do? Silence, a month. Then a call…divorce attorney.

Attorney, sternly, "Is there any chance of reconciliation, Mr. Benderoth? Marriage therapy?"

"No," I reply. Selfish fuck again. I choose career over Krista.

Attorney, coldly, "You will receive papers in the mail."

Special delivery, next day. She could have gone for adultery but chooses irreconcilable differences. No alimony. So, Krista. I'm ashamed. Not enough. Driven, obsessed. Put it behind me? I callously do.

Face a new life as a free man. I mix in with Bob's crowd. Party. Work. Work. Party. I move into a bigger apartment. I enjoy my many one-night liaisons. Finally, after two years, I'm a full-time editor. Five hundred a week. If I can make it here, thanks for the encouragement Mr. Sinatra. I get antsy.

Year and a half after the divorce, the holidays, and a visit home. Shopping for gifts with my younger sister Mindy and her daughter, Karis, my favorite niece. We go to a well-known, quaint tiny town, Ellicott City, Maryland. Reasonably priced antiques and crafts. Spot at a cute shop. Original stained-glass figures of popular icons stand out in the store front window, Snoopy, dead enter. Snoopy is my all-time favorite. I sneak away from Mindy and Karis. The proprietors, two young charming, friendly women.

Me, "Your shop is so cool. Never seen stained glass like this before. Please show me everything you have."

We chat for a time. Cindy, the shop owner, takes me into a back room. Story characters dangling, Mickey Mouse, Casper, Scooby Doo. One enchants me, a spider web with an adorable, smiling spider, Charlotte in her web. Perfect.

Cindy, "Apt choice, one of a kind."

Charlotte's Web is my niece's beloved bedtime story. "I'll take it."

Cindy, forwardly, "May I ask a personal question."

Me, "Ok. Shoot."

"Are you married? Not asking for me, Lisa and I are partners."

"Not now. Why?"

Cindy, "I have a friend. Single. I think you'd like each other. Can I give you her number?."

"I'm only in town for a couple of weeks, but sure."

I take the phone number, tuck stained glass "Charlotte" in my bag, start out. Damn. Forgot to ask the girl's name. Whatever.

Cindy, "Stop in again, Spider Guy. We exchange smiles. "Merry Christmas."

Me, way cool, "Back at ya."

I run. Catch up with Mindy and Karis.

Mindy, "That took a while."

"They were nice." Secretly show Charlotte. Whisper, "Karis."

Mindy hugging my arm, "Perfect."

We go to lunch, then home.

Christmas day, Mom's goes all out as usual. Big extended family party. Champagne flows. Feeling no pain. Again. Karis loves Charlotte, going to hang it in her bedroom window.

A few days pass. Bored, I remember the number Cindy gave me. I call.

Phone voice, "Hello?"

"This is out of the blue, but a friend of yours gave me your number. Thought we could meet. Coffee. Lunch."

"Well, Mick, Cindy told me Spider Guy would call."

I know this voice as well as I know my own. Krista Benderoth nee Felloni. I've been set up with my ex. Instant anxiety attack.

Krista, "I'm happy you reached out."

Happy? I don't think so.

Krista, "I have several things I never got the chance to tell you. It all happened so fast."

Fumbling, "Yes...fast. What...." Cuts me off dead.

Krista, "Fuck you! Fuck you!, Fuck you!, You immoral asshole!" CLICK! Not the Krista I once knew.

Payback is vicious...but just.

Dream Job

New York City, 1969. I had been here for six months. Broke, jobless, I was ready to pack it in when fate smiled. I landed a low paying apprenticeship at a tv commercial editing firm. A young filmmaker's dream.

One morning, when I got to work, I noticed a man and woman talking to my boss. The woman held an unlit cigarette between her slim, leather gloved fingers. My boss rushed to light it, she backed away.

"I gave it up. This is my pacifier."

She was dressed to the nines in a faux leopard short, short skirt, beige silk blouse, and high heeled Italian shoes. Mesmerized. I could not take my eyes off this incomprehensibly unique, iconic, eclectic, sexy woman standing before me. The man, her husband I soon discovered, wore rumpled, baggy khakis, a plaid flannel shirt, and Keds canvas sneakers.

My boss introduced me, "Mick, this is Arnold and Nancy Perl."

Arnold Perl? His name touched a nerve, a college drama class, a phrase in a textbook, *Tevye and His Daughters* a play that became the Broadway hit *Fiddler on the Roof.* What was this well-known playwright and his wife doing in a TV commercial editing house?

Arnold said, "I'm making a documentary on Malcolm X."

Malcolm who? I had no idea who he was talking about.

My boss cut in, "That black guy who got killed?"

"Assassinated," Nancy said curtly, "We have several thousand feet of TV news film that needs to be catalogued."

My boss started to reply, "We only edit TV comm..."

Nancy cut him off. "Warner Brother's is financing the film. I think we can make it worth your while."

Ever money-minded, my boss pointed to me, saying, "You can work with Mick, my apprentice." The deal was struck.

Arnold smiled at me rasping, "We'll start in the morning."

Whoa momma. Fate is smiling at me.

Months passed as we organized the footage. Arnold lit one cigarette after another. When I opened the door to get some air, smoke billowed out like a London fog. They worked in shifts. When Arnold was working on the script, I worked with Nancy. We worked together, bonding quickly...closer. A spark? Dream on, boy.

Lunch with Arnold, a Nathan's hot dog, soggy fries, and a Cel-Ray cream soda. Yuck, then back to work. With Nancy it was leisurely meals at bistros and upscale restaurants. Nancy ordered. I ate.

Once, waiting until I finished my first course, she asked, "What did you think of the snails?"

"Exquisite."

She took me to galleries, museums, avant-garde plays, foreign films. She taught. I learned. And so it went.

Biting into a French fry one day, Arnold casually asked me, "How would you like to edit the film, Mick?" This would change my life forever. His teaching was intense. A master's course in dramatic structure.

We worked 24/7 for a full year. The film was two-thirds finished. Arnold's cough was incessant, sometimes bringing him to his knees. He went right on working, smoking, working, smoking.

Nancy called me early one morning. "You sitting down?" A pause. "Arnold's dead. Heart attack. Please come down. I need you."

I staggered into a chair. I'm devastated. Crying, crying. I cannot stop. Arnold, my sage, my mentor, my dear, dear friend. Dead? Gone? My mind is fractured. I compose myself best I can. Take a cab down to Arnold and Nancy's brownstone. Arnold and Nancy's? No longer. Nancy. Alone.

Nancy opens the door. Fall into each other's arms. Her eyes as red as mine.

Through her sobbing she says, "Warner Brother's producer, Marvin Worth is on the phone. He wants to know who is going to finish *Malcolm X.*" Callous bastards. Arnold has not been gone a day. Nancy cannot speak, holds the phone out to me. The words pop right out of my mouth, surprising me.

"We are." I say to Worth, commandingly. "Nancy and I will finish Arnold's film."

Mavin Worth, not missing an insensitive beat, "Get out here now. I want to keep my eye on you."

The California sun blinded me as I walked down the steps of the jetliner that flew us from New York City to Los Angeles. A limousine drove us to the Chateau Mormont, a funky landmark hotel in Hollywood frequented by filmmakers and rock stars, from Scorsese to Jagger. The 'us' was my boss Nancy Perl and me.

Nancy checked us in, a fashion icon, her trademark un-lit cigarette ever in her hand, wearing oversized sunglasses. In Hollywood. Working on a studio film. I truly made it. Working with Arnold was a turning point in my life. He became my teacher and mentor. His sudden death left his dream unfinished. Warner Brothers was financing the film and agreed to let Nancy and me complete it. Nancy was the producer; I was the editor.

Nancy knew Hollywood like a native. After a long day's work, we would go to the Marmont pool for some sun and a quick dip. Nancy held her unlit cigarette between slim fingers. A guy with long black hair moves in to give her a light.

"May I, love?" he asks in a thick British accent.

Nancy smiles, "No thanks, I only hold."

He strolls away chuckling to himself. Another guy, red brown hair wind-blown joins him. Oh my God. It's Mick Jagger. The other dude was Ron Wood. Charlie soon joins his chaps. The Rolling Stones are crashing at the Mormont. Yes, Virginia, there is a film God.

After a shower and a change of clothes—for Nancy one of her eclectic outfits; for me a clean pair of jeans and tee shirt—we headed for the Strip, Sunset Strip, known for its music clubs and high-end restaurants. Sushi was de rigueur, with lots of sake. Nancy beelines for the Troub, the Troubadour, renowned, jam-packed rock club where Joni Mitchell, The Jefferson Airplane, The Stones, Lovin' Spoonful, often gigged. We saw em' all. R & R heaven.

Nancy had a coterie of friends, mostly actors, who had worked with her husband Arnold way back when he wrote for TV. We often spent long nights yapping wild stories, fueled by cocaine, marijuana and cognac that fueled up for all-nighters. Mornings, dazed, spaced, and back to the editing room. Days became months.

One night, after a nervous, grueling day of screening the film for Warner's executives, we crawled back to the Marmont burnt to a crisp. I followed Nancy to her room for a last puff. Stoned to the gills, I managed to stand up to go back to my room.

"Where are you going?" she purred.

By morning, we were a couple. Inseparable and loving it.

Back in New York, the film opened to solid reviews. It was nominated for an Academy Award, later bought by Spike Lee as the basis for his dramatic version starring Denzel Washington as Malcolm X. Arnold Perl's legacy added another feather to his posthumous cap.

Dream job triumphant.

Hubris

Heroes. Nancy and I return to NYC from Hollywood victorious, with a Warner Bros. Academy Award Nominated documentary, *"Malcolm X"* under our arms. Nancy ecstatic, "We're besieged with offers. We'll start a documentary company, Benderoth/Perl Productions. Our golden opportunity, baby." She throws her arms around me, then slowly pulls away, sensing something awry. Knows me all too well, "What's wrong?"

"I don't want to do any more documentaries." *Did I really say that? Sadly, yes, I did.*

Nancy's shocked, "What…what? This is a dream come true."

Me, pompously, "Not my dream." I pull a manuscript from my leather saddle bag like unsheathing a sword, "This is my dream."

Nancy, "A screenplay? When did you write that?"

"Every free second I had since I got to New York." I blurt out the title, "Brainchild. My modern take on the Universal Boris Karloff classic. I'm going to use the momentum from "Malcolm X" to make my dream happen."

I'm heating up at the sound of my own voice.

"Totally original. Unique." *I sense an ego problem coming on. Could be wrong.* "A psychotic high school science geek, weird right down to the oversized black shoes that squeak when he walks, making girls point and titter. He's obsessed with the bizarre idea of bringing dead things back to life. He does, loses control, is destroyed by his own monster. A natural. It can't lose." *Not wrong. Ego. Hubris. Naive squared.*

Nancy, placating, "Has anyone read it?"

Me, choking on my own words, "No, no, no, I want you to be the first. My gift to us." Gift? *Gift? Looking back, man, was I ever full of myself. Full of something else too. Nix the toilet humor.*

I hand it to her as if it was the tablets of the Ten Commandments. She takes, reads, while I wait for her to plop a laurel wreath atop my head.

Hours later no wreath forthcoming. "So?"

Nancy, "Well…"

Me, pushing, pushing, "Well, well, well what?"

Nancy, candidly, gently, "I think it's a pretty good first draft."

I lose it, "First draft! I've rewritten it ten times. It's finished. My final draft. It's my shooting script. Ready to go." *Oh dear, oh dear, oh dear. Hubris cubed.*

Nancy softly, not trying to further ignite me, "It might be a help to get feedback from some professional screenwriters.'

Me snidely, "Like Arnold's old buddies? They won't be hip to my style." *Can I believe the ass I was. Hip, style. Yuck!*

Nancy, "Just a suggestion. Might help polish your script."

Polish? Polish. I liked the sound of polish. "Yeah, get some seasoned pros to help me punch it up."

It gets punched alright: Left, right, left, right. Left.

One after another, kind, sincere, honest comments… 'this opening doesn't seem to work'…'story line could be stronger'… 'no foreshadowing', I didn't even know what that means. The final uppercut… 'It's just not there yet, Mick, but it's a good idea.' Idea! Idea! It's a friggin complete script. A screenplay. Not some friggin idea. These supposed pros smilingly hand back my precious manuscript. Parting shot, 'Best of luck.' *Hubris. Deaf, Dumb, no, not clinically dumb, talks a great game. Just dumb. Blind. I was nearsighted, but my glasses won't help me see what's right in front of me. Blind.*

Did I heed these words of wisdom? Nada, Niente, Nix, Nyet. No, fool. This is my shooting script, sacred, ready to be shot. Shoot the writer, now, please.

I face Nancy almost pounding my chest gorilla style. "I wrote it, I'll direct it, you'll produce it. I have five grand I saved from the Malcom film. I'll borrow another ten from my father.

Nancy, "I'm not sure you can make a film for so little…"

"I thought you could front me twenty grand." Overzealous, "You'll make it back two time over when investors see the rough cut. Trust me." *Trust me, the two most oft-spoken words in the film business. Save for, 'The checks in the mail…and 'I won't…' I'll keep it clean.*

Nancy, ever supportive of her children, she has two young daughters, Rebecca 11, Sarah 9…and me her little man child. My angel takes a leap of faith. "It's your ball game, Mick." I pick her little self up, swing her round the room. "Now my dream is coming true. *Hubris Ad Nauseum. Ralph! Ralph! Earl!, Earl!, Barf, no bag.*

So, first on my to do list, put together a crew, with little cash to afford one. I call in a lot of favors. It still left one crucial member. A cameraman. I viewed a lot of reels, all the good ones out of my league. A friend of a friend from Berkeley told Nancy of an up-and-coming shooter with solid creds, shot a couple no-budget features, knows the ropes. Robbie Greenberg. I gave him a call. He had a deep gruff but friendly voice. Robbie, "Send me your script,

I'll send you my sample reel." Robbie's' reel blows me away. Natural light, very Bergmanesque. Clearly, he knew how to light and shoot a film on a shoestring, but…Me, "Uh, how did you like the script, Robbie?'

Well…"

More wells. *The kid's drilling for water.*

Robbie, "I like it. Needs some tweaks, but it can work. I get $500 a week cash end of each shoot day….and you fly me out and back." The deal was done.

Now cast. Nancy praised a pro casting director, dear friend, but no, I wanted to hand pick the actors for my roles. *Fool rushing.*

My cast in place, I plan to shoot in East Hampton, Nancy's house, our production office. We'll scout and nail locations out there. Nancy's buds. Gratis for sure. *Total user. Users use up.*

Robbie made the crew toe the line. Sweltering summer sun, twelve-hour days, dragging butts home…crash.

Me on the other hand in heaven. Best summer ever. What could possibly go wrong? How could I lose? *Infamous last words.*

Four weeks later "Brainchild" was in the can. "It's a wrap, I yell." The crew cheers, my arms thrust in air like Rocky Balboa. *Oh, brother. More like rocky bottom.*

We move back to New York for editing, my forte. Piece of cake. I dive in. *The deep end. Not a great swimmer. I tread…then sink, hit bottom.*

Halfway through the rough cut, truth slams me in the gut. Flickering right in front of my face on the editing screen. Can this be the film I directed? Oh no, Joe, tell me it ain't so. Joe. So. All the unheeded wisdom that floated in one, out the other, lay before me. I can save my baby, top of the line editor. I can give it life. *Just like the kid in his movie, the film, his monster, malformed, out to kill.* I recut, recut, recut. Showbiz reality hits me between the eyes, "You can't polish a turd."

"Brainchild." Brain dead.

Screening after screening for possible investors like a viewing at the old filmmaker's funeral home for dead movies. From hero to zero. I saw my career flushed like my big brown turd down the toilet.

I hide in my office for a year doing nothing. Couldn't get a gofers job. I rode my momentum to nowhere. Which is where I was. *Square one to the nth.*

Nancy's brownstone. While I licked my wounds in my upstairs office, things were cooking downstairs. Next year was

1976. Philadelphia was building a Bicentennial Museum. Nancy got the prime job producing a film on the "Bill of Rights" with a budget of over three hundred grand, Mega money for a thirty-minute short. She hires the best of the best, set, costume, make up…all her pals from New York to Hollywood plus…a top Broadway director to helm the epic. Then…a phone call.

I hear Nancy slowly climb the stairs to my office, saunters in. I stand, give a hug and kiss, "Hey, baby, how's it going?"

"Fucked. We lost our director."

"What? He was so hot on the job."

"Broadway called. He answered."

"Gonna be tough to find someone else so close to production."

"Already got one."

"Fast, even for you. Anybody I know?"

"I think you do."

"Yeah?"

"You."

"Me?" I'm shocked, flabbergasted. Speechless. *Which is still unusual for me. Even now. Fifty years later.*

Nancy, grinning, "Yes. You."

Me, a dizzy, shaky, "I…I don't know, Nancy, you've got a lot riding on this. I'm not sure…"

"I am."

I never worked so hard in my life listening, heeding, learning, from seasoned pros. The production went smooth as silk. It was the hit of the Bicentennial Museum.

From hero, to has been, to hero all because a woman who loved and trusted me, gave me a second chance. *Humility enter stage right. Hubris exit stage left. Finis.*

Chutzpah

Marty Starrman had something I didn't. Chutzpah. Essential in Hollywood.

Brash. He could insinuate himself into anything, anyplace, anytime. Armed guards and stone-faced secretaries could not deter him. Unstoppable. Obnoxious, yes. Hustler, yes. Smart, yes. Charm, maybe? Oozing what? Ethics? No. But we needed each other. A team. It worked until it didn't.

My savvy wife and business partner, Nancy and I first encountered Marty in the hall outside my editing room in New York City's Film Center Building. We were finishing up a TV commercial. Just getting off the elevator, Starrman was well put together, a tailored blazer, tailored slacks, monogrammed shirt, and Italian loafers.

Nancy whispers to me, "Take a gander at that jerk. No socks. No damn socks. Uggh! Tasteless West Coast."

Mrs. Caveat Emptor. I shrug off Nancy assessment. But I would pay for not heeding her unerring first take on people. My bad, yet again

"Hey, dude, you must be Mick Benderoth. Just coming to see you. I'm Marty Starrman. I work with Bob Franks. Raising money for Frank's way hot movie magazine, *Variety*, New York style." Hand out.

We shake. But way hot? LA buzz word. Another missed clue.

"Frank's already tapped us. No sale." Nancy smirks.

163

Marty, smooth as, well, Marty, "Not here to hustle ya, dudes. Frank says Mick's got a dynamite screenplay, way commercial, *Street Smart*. Killer title. Who's your agent, dude? Who's he shown it to?"

Way too many dudes. Too many friggin' questions, too fast. Keeps firing. "Want a read? Got connections in Hollywood. Maybe I can help."

Nancy senses I'm not heeding her warning. "I'll meet you in the café downstairs. When you're finished with Mr. Dude."

She hops the next elevator leaving me alone. Am I a sap or what?

Marty, "So, Dude, let's do lunch."

Do lunch? Yes, yet another missed clue. C'mon, Mick, shake duddy.

Marty, undaunted, "Free tomorrow?"

Me thinks the dude persists too much. "Give me a copy of your script."

"No good. Client meeting." I turn away.

"Day after? Whenever. I'm free the rest of my week. I'll track you down. Here's my card, BB slipped me yours. Gotta runs. Later, dude."

Much later. I run to my editing room. Door closed.

Marty calls and calls. Filibusters. Me? A sap. I fold.

"Russian Tea Room?"

"Fine."

"I'll make us a rez, dude. Oneish?"

Oneish? Oneish? Signal overload. Cut me some slack, dude. "Fine."

Marty, emphatic, "Don't forget that way hot script, dude." Click.

Russian Tea Room, Marty seated. He flashes me his signature Cheshire Cat smile. I sit.

Marty snaps his finger to a waiter, calls. "Hey, dude, we need drinks here."

Another signal. Not Cool. I'm such a mark. Still, I actually end up enjoying his company. Seduced? I give him my script. We part.

"Be in touch, Buddy."

Buddy? Hell, I just met this dude.

A couple of weeks later, I meet Bob Franks in the lobby. Marty's back in LA. for his mag. Weeks fly by. Marty Starrman, out of sight, out of, you know, whatever.

Sunday morning, early. Way too early. Nancy and I, post coital haze. I take the call. It's him.

"Hey, Dude."

"It's Mick. I prefer Mick."

"Sure, man, Mick."

"Been a while since we…." Cuts me off.

Rapid fire. "You know Roger Corman, producer who made all those Edgar Allen Poe B-horror flicks. He wants to get into TV. I got a leg up."

Leg up? What?

"Roger hired a friend of mine as head of TV production, Lynn Travis. Not bad in bed."

Oh my. Way too much information.

"Lynn's looking for a two-hour pilot script. Showed her yours. Not what Roger's looking for, but Lynn said she'll run it by features. No promises."

Now I'm listening, "Great, thanks."

"Hold on, du…ah Mick. Gets better. She likes your style. Corman's looking for something ala *Dukes of Hazzard*, the TV series."

Me, proudly, "Never saw it."

Starrman's on a roll, "Sexy chicks, cool guys, down south, car chases. You know the scene. Come up with an idea, I'll run it by Lynn. Interested? We got nothing to lose but our appetites."

Oh, brother.

"Call me when you have something." Click.

165

Am I really doing this? Lying in bed brainstorming. I am. Poor writers…so vulnerable. A phrase pops into my head. *Georgia Peaches.* I keep storming. Two Georgia sisters, the Peaches, Sue Lynn, waitress in a dive, Terry Lee, grease monkey, car savant, both adorable, looking for a way up. Enter Dusty Tyree, flip, handsome, hustler, running moonshine in hidden tanks in the back of his Mustang, cops in hot pursuit. Take out line, "I can outrun anything…except a bullet."

I fly it by Marty. "You sold *me*, Mick. Ya nailed it, Write *me* a couple of pages. UPS *me*. I'll pitch it to Lo."

Helpless sappy writers. I write the pages, UPS 'em to Marty Starrman. What have I got to lose? Famous last…

Four weeks. Nothing. Then LA dude rears his head. On the phone. Hyperventilating,

"Lynn loves it. Showed it to Corman. Wants to meet the writers ASAP." Writers? What writers?

Me, pissed, "They want to bring in other writers to develop my story into a script! No way in hell am I gonna…"

"Easy, Du…ah, Mick. Writers…you and me, Benderoth/Starrman…a team."

I should have expected a "what's in it for me." Well, here it is. He did do the leg work. Marty's leg was always up. Chutzpah.

Mick the schmuck gives in. Mick and Marty…screenwriters. Queasy.

Marty, still racing, "When can you get out here?"

Out here? Oh, boy. Nancy's gonna love this.

Back home in New York City, after a year in Hollywood, Nancy's back at the top of her game, a coveted high end TV commercial producer, and back to her first love, painting. She's happy. I'm not. The taste of Hollywood lingers. I have to go. *Carpe diem* again.

Nancy, always supportive, "Go for it, Baby. But this guy Marty?"

Why do I not listen to her? She's smarter, more savvy, more everything then I will ever be. Nancy's been there, done that. Why do I not listen to my Goddess of wisdom? *Way, way, way, more why.*

I fly out. Marty in the lounge, Veuve Cliquot in one hand, two flutes, the other. Cracks it then, there. Clink!

"To us." Us? Get used to it...Dude.

Corman loves *Georgia Peaches.* Orders a script on the spot. Unheard of.

Marty explodes.

"We got heat! Gotta moves before it cools."

He gets us an agent at Wm. Morris. I begin my Hollywood career...with my partner Monty Starrman, long on talk and short on writing. Me, clueless.

I toss ideas. Marty sets up meetings. Producers, TV development dudes, dudettes, pitching in tandem, loving it.

We...I write like a fool. Didn't I call myself a fool before? Anyhoo. Lynn calls. Corman gives *Peaches* a green light. Triple unheard of! Our friggin script is going to get made. Hallelujah! Celebrate! Celebrate! Years before Madonna. Ma Mason, ultra-high-end Hollywood eatery. Orson Welles frequents, two chairs put together. Then I revisit The Strip. Clubs till early morning. Drunk. Delirious. I cab back to my hotel and crash.

New life. Write, pitch, write, pitch, write, pitch. Happiness. *Tempus fugit.*

Marty says he's going away for the weekend. Comes back with his hot new bride, Allegra Mandrega.

Me, overly surprised, "Congratulations."

"Thank you...Mick?" she says.

I nod. "Marty has said so many good things about you, but please excuse me, I must run. A meeting."

To Marty Allegra says, "See you down the hill later, Marty my darling?"

"After we work a while." They kiss. Allegra departs, squealing off in her Jaguar. Jaguar?

Marty, "Seems fast I know, but we've been seeing each other for a while." He dishes. Allegra's ex- is a wealthy Argentinian banker. She's loaded and wants a new life in Tinseltown. Did he really say Tinseltown? Allegra needs a green card, a sponsor. You guessed it, "Marty, my darling." Ethics slippery, he moves in with her. I take over his apartment.

Wonderous news. *Peaches* debut is scheduled on CBS.

I fly home to be with Nancy for *Peaches* premier. She surprises me with a party. Our closest pals watching *Georgia Peaches,* in color on TV. It don't get no better than this.

Now, the biggest pitch of my life. Getting Nancy to move out to LA. "Nancy, Marty and I are... hot..."

Hot? Did I actually say that word? Nancy my darling, forgive me.

She's not crazy about going back, but signs on for a year, makes a few calls, lines up a few producing gigs. We rent out our brownstone. She finds a huge, two bedroom LA apartment on Vine Street. Yes, yes, that's right, just up the hill from the legendary, Hollywood and Vine. Crossroads where dreams come true, or not. *Georgia Peaches* pilot is not picked up. Downer? Not to Marty.

"We can still fly on the heat, dude." Please, no, no. no.

So, flyin' on some kinda heat or something, Marty and I pitch our brains out, have some luck landing a few script deals. Soon, I'm doing re-writes of re-writes of re-writes, other writer's crappy stuff for tweaking... Development Hell. Up to my neck. Nothing gets made. One trick ponies? I stick in.

Nancy and I hold my traditional St. Patty's Day party. Me, a "mick" Mick. Half Irish. Corned beef and cabbage. Guinness on tap. I invite new friends and biz contacts for networking, another Hollywood must. We're mobbed. A free meal pulls 'em in.

Marty shows with Allegra and her best friend, Elena. I notice them frequenting the bathroom. A quiet aside, "You guys using the john a lot...coke?."

Marty whispers, "Sex. Green card pussy. Fucking both. The ladies are gay. Lovers. In heaven, dude."

Marty ethics...none.

A year turns into five. Nancy antsy. Antsy Nancy not good. I'm burnt, disillusioned, disgusted with me.

Marty shows up for a pitch, very, very pale. "Talk later. Take the lead."

I do. He sits it out. After... "She told me to move out. Wants to live alone with Elena. Vegas divorce—I was conned."

The conner conned. Whoa. He's dead broke. Hits me for a loan. I give. Keeps hitting. Then, the kicker. Without warning, the son of a bitch breaks our team, takes a job as a development exec at CBS. Mutiny. I am pissed. He's the reason I'm here. His friggin *chutzpah*. This time used for himself. Has it always been this way? He sweet talks. Promises, promises. Total access to CBS. He'll get me a deal. Never happens. Actually, stops taking my calls. Friendship? Were we ever? Fool me once...you know the rest. I give lone wolfing a try. Bleaker and bleaker. *Genug!* Enough.

Nancy rushes me back to the sanctuary of our East Hampton beach house. Double dazed, I stop writing, thinking, being. Salvation. A tip from my therapist gets me into a playwriting group at Guild Hall, East Hampton's famed art complex. The stage, an unknown landscape. Yet again, Nancy covers my back. I dive in. Months and months of writing. This time for me. I finish a play. It gets accepted. Nancy takes hold, producing, costumes, calling in favors from old buddies. They handle sets and lighting. Raves. Success. Playwright. Reinvention. True happiness.

You got it. The phone rings.

That's right, him...again.

169

"Hey, how's it goin' dude?"

How soon they forget.

Me heavy, "Mick, no dude."

"Right, Mick. I got a leg up."

Frigging leg up…again.

Spiel, "CBS and Showtime are partnering, a three MOW deal." MOW, movie of the week. "CBS wants in on cable. Showtime's their way. We need a story."

We? Fool on the hill. I bite. Hook line, whatever. I'm addicted. Can't get this monkey off my back. Not telling Nancy.

I come up with, a story, an urban legend. Bodies found in garbage dumps. Eviscerated. Transplant black market. A murder victim's the organ source. Young female cop, Deidre. Her father on a long list for kidney transplant, the rich at the head of the line, buying pirate organs. Deidre solves the case. Title, *Vital Parts*.

Marty pitches. Showtime.

"Yes!" Marty's reframe,

"Get out here now!"

Nancy, no fucking way. Ecstatically back to painting, Show in the works. Her words to the not so wise, "Big fish, small pond is small fish in big pond. Regional theaters chafing at the bit for you, directing your work. Do you really need this? Think hard, Mickey." Nancy only calls me Mickey when she's deadly earnest.

I can't get this monkey off my back. "I'll…I'll commute."

Nancy, unsmiling, "I'll try it out."

I ping pong from NY to LA for weeks, exhausted, Nancy's way past unhappy. Ultimatum. "Me or Hollywood, your call."

Self-destruction's my middle name. Addicted. "Nanc…?"

Cuts me off harshly, "Good luck, goodbye…Mickey."

Breakup? Breakup. Period. She walks out, drives back to the city. Fools rush in.

I fly and crash at Marty's. What is wrong with me? Faust? Marty on the phone. Covers the mouthpiece.

Wide-eyed, hissing, "Showtime wants a draft of 'Vital'…pronto!."

Pronto? Lone Ranger, me Tonto?

We…I…work 24/7. Submit. CBS and Showtime have notes. One wants red one wants blue. Rewrite schizoid. Marty, cash poor again, submits unfinished draft behind my back to trigger payment. Ethics, never.

CBS/Showtime pass. *Vital Parts* is dead in the water.

I left a queen in paradise, for what? Me, heartsick. Marty leads, I follow. Numb. Pitch. Nothing, *nada, nuente.* I'm fried. Tequila in the freezer. Pass out.

Marty, way too loud. "Mick. Mick. Yo Mick! Phone. Nancy."

Nancy? Nancy!

"Mick…" At least not Mickey. "Thinking about you…a lot."

Heart pounding.

Nancy, "How are you holding up?"

Her voice. I break. Stream of consciousness babble. Pitiful.

Nancy, out of left field, "I think we should get married."

What? What? What? Hell to heaven. Incomprehensible.

Nancy coos, "Baby, time to come home."

The red eye…home.

Married in EH house on Christmas Eve. Bliss. Finally.

Time passes. Two more plays under my belt.

Phone call.

Friggin' Marty. No greeting. He jumps right into it. "Dude, running hit TV series looking for new blood. Our agent knows the exec producer. Hawked for us. Way interested. Our dream job. Hirable ever after. Run out while the door's wide open, dude."

"Slam it!"

"What?"

"Not interested."

Marty, "Our golden opportunity!"

"I'm already living my golden opportunity.

"Dude...Mick...you're talking crazy."

"Crazy maybe. But happy crazy.

"Come on..."

"Goodbye Marty."

"Goodbye?."

"And good luck."

"Mick...Mick. Mick..."

"A favor."

"Favor? Anything...anything."

"Marty, put your ear very, very close to the phone and listen for a change. Don't ever, ever, ever fucking call me again, dude. Click!"

Chutzpah!

Taormina

I wiped the sleep from my eyes. My vision cleared. I stared up at a white stucco ceiling. It took me a moment to realize where I was. A warm breeze blew a sweet smell into the room and with it a flood of memories. It was salty sea air. I got out of bed and walked through the open sliding glass doors onto a terrace. My feet felt hot. I looked down to see terracotta tiles heated by sun. I walked to the edge of the terrace, seeing what I had only dreamed of. The sea, the Mediterranean Sea. I was transfixed. I was in Sicily.

I felt a soft hand on my shoulder. I turned to see my wife Nancy smiling. She was reading my mind, "It had the same effect on me my first time."

"Thank you for sharing Taormina with me, my love."

We embrace, kiss deeply. The delicious kiss was salty. I realize this shapely, small creature was wearing her black leotard bathing suit.

"So, you've been for your morning swim without me *Nasty Nancy.*" My pet name for her.

"Put on your trunks. We'll go back in together. Come back for a hot shower, then…"

She pecked me impishly on my lips, grinning her seductive Nancy grin that meant only one thing. I was already aroused, seeing my water nymph in her skintight dark royal purple leotard, now I was fully. So, with the promise of love making *après* swimming, I was fully.

She touched me, teased me, "Save that for later darling."

Another kiss, then to the pebbled beach. A swim with the love of your life in a mythical body of water, showering together, as your sweet passionate ritual begins, finished upon a silk sheeted bed in a magical Sicilian realm. Life cannot possibly be any finer.

A knock at the door. Breakfast!," Nancy cooed in my ear.

I don my white terrycloth robe, stroll to and open the door. Standing there, dressed in a crisp white coat was a handsome young waiter with a tray filled with fresh brioche, a huge chunk of butter, various jams and jellies and a silver pot of hot coffee.

The waiter walked onto the terrace, setting our morning meal on a marble table.

"No bacon and eggs here sweetheart. This is breakfast European style." My first trip to Europe, overanxious to explore, I lusted for it all. Including Nancy. After a humorous explanation of a bidet, we were off to the town of Taormina. The reason we took the bumpy flight from Italy. Taormina. What can I say? The pearl of the Mediterranean. It was 1977 and had not yet become an overcrowded tourist attraction.

This town on a hill with stone houses, cobblestone streets, and tiny shops, was overshadowed by Mt. Etna, the active volcano smoldering in the background. Clouds billowed in an azure sky. The sun still in command. In Taormina, a Catholic ceremony welcoming Spring, had taken over. At the front of the church procession were four young girls dressed in white dresses, carrying nosegays.

Camera to my eye, I focused on the girl up front. She smiled, blushed, I snapped the shutter, capturing a memorable photograph that still hangs over my desk.

Nancy hugged me around my waist from behind as we rode the funicular, an old cable car, as it crawled up the town's mountain side. The front window framed Taormina growing larger and larger until it lay before us. Nonnis, in their black shawls stood protectively in their stone front doorways.

The shops beckoning my shopping addicted wife she takes my hand pulling,. "C'mon, baby. Let's explore."

We hit every shop, presents for her two daughters, Rebecca and Sarah, her beloved mother Annabel, a woman I adored almost as much as Nancy. Plus, sandals for us, and a hand-woven straw hat I plopped on her tiny head.

"You like?" I asked.

She turns, backs away to frame herself in a tarnished mirror on the shot wall.

"I love," she said skipping away childlike, a head turn back to me, "C'mon Mickey. Hurry. There's more, then lunch at a place Lidia told me about."

I would follow this elf anyplace and do so for many years. My adorable, smart, sassy playmate.

We took the funicular back down to the beach. Dusk was settling in. Landing on the pristine beach, we met fishermen bringing in the days catch. Locals bargained for what would be our dinner in a restaurant called Pesche, situated at the end of a long pier, that our concierge recommended. I had a platter of fresh sea urchins, treacherous spikes guarding the delicacy inside. I scooped out the sumptuous, creamy roe. It tasted of the Mediterranean Sea. I was in heaven.

The next morning, still glowing from yesterday, we drove to the Teatro Antico di Taormina, a Greco-Roman theater still used today. We meandered through this magical place, and I felt a spell cast over me. Aeschylus, Euripides, Sophocles echoed in my mind.

We ambled through the town, passing houses that seemed carved in rock. The locals were gracious and forthcoming, as we bought souvenirs from street vendors.

Sad that our time here was fast coming to an end, we went down to the beach. I picked up a stone and handed it to Nancy. "Our Taormina," she said, slipping it into her pocket. We walked back to the funicular and glided up to the town to catch our flight back to Italy.

Years later, I look at the photograph of the young girl, standing at the top of the stone stairway, still smiling at me, pulling me into the picture, back to Taormina, the pearl of the Mediterranean. And still standing beside me, Nancy, my very own pearl.

Kick The Cane

Visiting my parents in Baltimore wasn't on my top ten list. I had major issues with my father. He was undergoing chemotherapy and radiation for recurring prostate cancer with complications, so my mother's call urged me to make the trip from New York City, where I now lived.

My father was asleep when I arrived. Mom gave me dinner and filled me in. Cancer had metastasized to his lymph glands. He had stopped working, hard for a relentless workaholic. Mom was caring for him at home.

Exhausted from driving, I crashed in the bedroom where my brother Steve and I grew up. Nothing changed. Like I never left. Unsettling.

Something woke me. I heard grunts, splashes, whimpers, from the hall bathroom. I jumped up to see what was going on. It was four in the morning. Dad's bed was empty. I knocked on the bathroom door.

"Dad, Dad are you ok?"

"Mick is that you? Come on in, I need some help."

I opened the door and saw my dad in the bathtub, shocked at how this once muscular 250-pound man was now skin and bones.

He wheezed, "I wanted to take a bath. I got in ok, but I can't get out."

"Let me help you." I reached under his arms, locking my hands behind his back. "Try to stand as I lift."

After a few tries, he got to his feet. I held tightly as he lifted his sinewy legs out of the tub. He was shivering and exhausted. I sat him on the toilet seat.

"Thank God you're here, Mick. I don't know what I would have done without you."

First time ever he asked for my help. My father in severe need, I am his oldest son, my heart went out to him. I dried him off, staring into his fearful, sad blues eyes, once strong and fierce. Memories roiled through my mind.

Me, eight, Steve, seven, playfully wrestling with Dad on the living room floor. We rolled him over and plopped across his body.

"We win!" Steve shouted. Dad's eyes widened. A devilish grin formed on his face. In a flash of brute strength, he flips us on our backs, kneeling over us, putting a massive hand on the center of our chests, pinning us down.

His grin more devilish, "The only way you two will ever take me is when I'm walking with a cane, and you kick the cane out from under me." A taunt never forgotten.

My father was a depression era kid whose only way out of poverty was to join the US Navy, proudly wearing his Navy hat at the popular jaunty angle. A true Horatio Alger hero. He pulled himself up from blue collar roots, becoming a successful restaurateur. A workaholic, he was never home, worked every weekend, Sunday included. We seldom saw him. But, after an unending plethora of 24/7 weeks, months, years, he burned out. Sold his thriving enterprise for big bucks. Workaholism soon set in again.

He got bored of home life, and surprising everyone, he bought a failing direct mail company. Again, he single-handedly turned it into a nationally known, thriving business, allowing my mother to raise his family in luxury. He was never home, again. The American dream come true. Dad works, mom, moms.

Home life with him was not such a dream. One Sunday dinner, table meticulously set with dishes of my father's favorites, caringly prepared by our mom. She said something. What? Who knows? Not me. Years later I can never remember a single one of the innocent pins once pulled, setting off my father's hand grenade tantrums. KABOOM! He grabs the edge of the tablecloth, yanks it and Sunday dinner off the table cascading through the dining room. Mashed potatoes, gravy oozing down the wallpaper. Red faced, blue eyes budging, he stomps out of the house, into his car and drives off, leaving his family in shock and awe, never to be mentioned again, lest it pull another pin.

He was not an affectionate man. I never saw him hug or kiss my mother, or say "I Love You," even on their anniversaries, always forgotten, but not on his birthday, which he expected to be celebrated with homemade cake, candles, presents, the song, the whole ego trip.

Then, there was his blame game, holding us accountable for anything that went wrong which we were in no way responsible for. It was always our fault. Period.

Our last explosive encounter, around my twenty fourth birthday, late sixties. I was teaching school, living at home far too long, saving money for my first trip to Europe. Yet there he was again standing before me, eyes bulging, red faced, fist raised to strike, for some self-perceived wrongdoing, bitterly hissing through clinched teeth.

"Flinch…just flinch and an inch!" I did not flinch an inch, believing that someday he might reach his tipping point and lash out physically. His parting shot. "You know what you are? You're a nothing, a nothing. That's what you are. Nothing."

Nothing? Is that truly what this troglodytic man thought of his oldest son? Nothing?. An ego stab I'd be dealing with in therapy the rest of my life fighting to lose the curse he laid upon me.

As usual, he turned in silence, stomping up the clubroom stairs, out the front door. Never apologized for harm he caused anyone, not me, my brother, nor my mother who got the brunt of it all.

It was the last time I saw him for years, moving to my own apartment, with no goodbyes, then on to New York, my new home.

A solemn Christmas, five years later. The whole family gathered. My father's cancer had moved to his brain, inoperable. My mother nursed him at home, driving him daily to the invasive, tortuous, chemo treatments that left him emaciated, colostomy and urine bags dangling, down to 125 pounds.

I went into his room, again shocked at his more diminished form. He slowly turned to face me smiling, as I bent down instinctively kissing him on the cheek.

"That's what I love about you, Mickey. You're not afraid to show your affection, always there with a hug or a kiss."

Love? A word I never heard him utter, never congratulating me on my accomplishments, nary a handshake. Enigmatic. Months later, a final visit to a hospice where dad had been moved when mom could no longer care for him. Our family assembled again, possibly for the last time. My father, now in a coma. His breathing was shallow, barely perceptible.

"I don't hear a pulse," the doctor said softly. "Breathing is the last to go."

I mentally counted every breath until the doctor pronounced my father dead.

In the end, it was not Steve, nor I who kicked his cane out from under our father, but cancer, a force he could not bully.

My father, a man I could never decipher nor unconditionally love. At seventy-seven, I am still trying.

String Bean

"Hi ya!" *Swish! Thrump.* "Alright!," I yell, my fist thrust in air, as I stand over my karate Sensei, Tsei, lying flat on the mat.

"Sorry master," I gloat. I offer her my hand.

"Hay Hi Yah Ruff!" *Thrump!*

Sensei now stands over me and says, "Hubris is our enemy, Gakusei."

I stand and bow, chastened. Tsei bows in return. She goes to her satchel takes out a purple belt looped over her hands, bows again. She unties my brown belt tosses it aside, puts the purple belt around my waist, ties it with a yank.

Tsei nods, smiling, "You earned it, you're the best student I've taught. Purple in two years. Now onto black."

"I will try, Sensei."

Tsei, sternly, "Not try. Will!"

I've been taking karate to bury the image that has followed me since high school, String Bean, geek.

I bike back to work in the video tape editing room. I'm freelance editing, finishing a TV news story as Fran, my boss approaches holding her cell.

"Here's a weird one, someone anonymously sent an email video to our citizen line, forwarded to me. A small town in Georgia, Gainesville. Take a look." Fran starts the video. A young's face woman, terrified.

"He's got the whole town scared to death. Nothing can stop him. He killed Blamer's dogs, cats, his whole chicken coop 'cause he didn't pay up. Burned out two trucks, Pritchard's, and Mr. Traner. Same thing, couldn't pay. We, we, need…"

A harsh voice cuts her off, "What the hell you doing with a cell, Marinda? You know they ain't allowed in town. Give it here."

A man's hand grabs it. We hear it crash to the ground. Loud foot stomp finishes it off. A beefy arm enters the frame. I see it and freak. The big red heart with a knife stuck in it is an image emblazoned in my mind. Memory flashes. I'm a tall, skinny, high school, thick-lensed, horn-rimmed glasses, straight A student, major bookworm. In essence, a nerd.

Ooofff! A well-worn, scuffed black military boot trips me, schoolbooks out of my hand, they go flying. Him again. Lester Hinchcliffe aka Flik, self-named after the gravity knife he carries. Flik laughs his snarky growl. "Haw! Haw! Haw!" He's been the school bully since middle school. Voted most hated in yearbook.

Built like a linebacker, he holds out his hand to me, "Lemme me help you, String Bean." The nickname he gave me. Big mistake number one. I stupidly take his hand. He flips me over his shoulder I slam onto the cold hall tile floor, his booted foot stomping my hand.

"Say it, String Bean."

He stomps harder. Don't think I can't hold out.

"Say it String Bean, Unless ya want yer hand smashed."

I will not give. Flik puts two hundred and fifty pounds on my hand.

I cave, screaming, "I worship the ground you walk on, master of the universe."

Flik slides his boot off my swollen hand, smirks, "Like scraping off dog shit."

I jump up fuming. I charge. Big mistake two. Swick! Flick! His blade out, touching my crotch. "Flinch, just flinch an inch, String Bean, I'll ruin your sex life forever."

I snap out of the memory. The man's hand grabs the cell. We hear it smash to the ground. A foot stomp crushes it, but not before the smart lady pressed send.

"He's Lester Hinchcliffe. Went to school with him."

Fran, "How do you know? No name, no face?"

"That tattoo. I'd know it anywhere. Lester Hinchcliffe, aka Flik, a creep who bullied us at Milford Mill High, in Maryland. I was Flik's prime target. He must have moved down south."

Fran, "How can one guy terrorize a whole town?"

That's the angle. "I know I'm not a reporter, but let me run with this, check it out. If it's anything, I'll send for a video crew."

Obsessed, I go to Gainesville, Georgia. It's hot. Way humid. I can hardly breathe the saturated air.

I ask at the gas station, "You know a guy named Lester Hinchcliffe?"

The station attendant's face blanches. He shakes head no. I go to get in my car. The attendant runs over to whisper harshly.

"He…he might be in the bar. Down Skiff Street. Left at the corner."

I pull up in front of the bar. Park. Get out, go in. Holy shit. It's him. The familiar knot in my gut squinches. Then see the badge on his shirt. So that's how he does it. He's the town Sherriff. Extorts the whole town for protection. Definitely a story here.

I yell to him, "Hey Flik!"

His head snaps, faces me, "Who the hell are you and what the hell ya want with me?"

"Don't remember me do you?"

"Can't say I do. Glad that I don't."

"We went to high school together."

Flik, ponders. Eyes pop. "String-fuckin-bean! School nerd. Hell, you haven't changed much, still a tall, skinny string bean. What you doin' way down here?"

"Passing through. Saw you. Just saying hi."

Flik, smirking, "Hi. Goodbye String Bean."

I walk outside, knowing I'll stick around till I get a story when it jumps up right in my face. A State Trooper's car pulls up outside the bar. The whole place goes silent.

Flik growls, "Now what do we have here?" He saunters out. Growls snidely, "Can I help you...Officer?"

State Trooper, "Someone called in a complaint about the Sheriff of Gainesville. Are you Lester Hinchcliffe?"

"That's me. Sheriff Hinchcliffe."

"That's the problem. State records show that no one named Lester Hinchcliffe is registered as sheriff of Gainesville or anywhere else."

Flik, "Is that so."

Speed of light. *Flick.* Knife out. *Swish! Thuck!* Buried deep in Trooper's chest. He gasps, drops.

Bartender, "You will never get away with..."

Flik cuts 'tender off with a back hand rap. Trooper lays there, out of it, groaning, bleeding. Flik takes the Trooper's gun, walks back up on the bar porch.

I run to the trooper. Pull off my tee shirt, push it on the trooper's wound.

Flik, "Back away string bean. You don't got no dog in this fight."

"Fuck you, Hinchcliffe. A police officer needs help." I pull out my cell. *Blam!* Hinchcliffe shoots it out of my hand, flesh wound.

Me, "You need a gun to deal with little old String Bean, Sheriff Hinchcliffe?"

Flik steams, "Well now. You grown some balls. Maybe a pistol whippin's just the ticket."

He rushes me, gun raised high. I kick higher, knock the gun out of his hand, catch it midair. Flik, shocked. Recovers.

"Nice trick, String Bean. What now? Gonna shoot me?

190

"I don't need a weapon to deal with a coward." I unload it. Drop shells and gun.

Flik now full tilt, nods to a crony who tosses him a pool cue. Flik snaps it in two, leaving him holding two sharp splintered weapons. He races at me chaotically, cues flailing.

I sidestep karate move, like a matador.

Flik whips by, slams into a truck. Turns, charges again.

High kick to his chin. The crowd gasps.

Flik lands on his back. Crazed. Jumps up. Mindlessly rages toward me again.

HEEE! AAAH! Me, airborne. Both my feet slam square in his chest. Sends him shattering through the bar window. Dazed.

I walk over to see his splayed hand on the ground. Flash back to the highs school hallway, Flik's booted foot grinding my hand into the marble floor. Flik, "Say it, String Bean, say it, Say it. Say it." The words echo in my brain.

I snap back to the present. Stare at Flick's hand. Serious temptation. I will not sink down into Flik's hateful realm.

He mumbles, "mumbles, "Fuckin String Bean." Collapses unconscious.

Late afternoon. Three State Trooper cruisers and an ambulance arrive. The wounded trooper on a gurney smiles as he passes me. I nod, smile back.

Flik in cuffs is shoved screaming into a patrol car. "String Bean, you shit. You'll never…"

Door slam. Window closed. I see, don't hear his twisted face mouth off.

"Last I heard about Flik, he had a rough time in stir. Guards found him naked on the cold shower room tile floor, his own flick gravity knife stuck deep in his chest, blood bubbling out of his mouth. Stabbed through his heart, just like the blood red tattoo on his budging bicep.

They said his last word, whispered, *"String Bean."*

Popie

Visiting my mother in the late seventies after my father passed was a treat. Good food and family reminiscences were a welcome diversion from my editing job in NYC. One morning she has a doctor's appointment, so I'm alone. I pick up two rubber hand balls I got from Amazon. I have some arthritis in my hands, my orthopedist said they would help. I plop on the bed, reading the local paper, as I squeeze the balls. One slips out of my hand, to the floor, rolls under the bed. I got up, kneel to retrieve it and see a box.

I slither under and pull it out. Sit on the floor, I open it. It is my collection of old home movies. 8mm film from before video, now chips. I dig in. My eye catches title, Popie, a man I hadn't thought about in years, my brother Steve and my step-grandfather, Popie, a man we loved dearly. I ferret out my old Keystone movie projector, dust it off, thread the reel up and watch the images on the bedroom wall. Steve and Popie were tossing a football at Fort McHenry on one of the many adventures with Popie while I captured it with my Kodak Brownie movie camera, as usual. Steve ten, me eleven. The Fort, a Baltimore Revolutionary War landmark, the place where Francis Scott Key scribbled The Star-Spangled Banner on the back of a parchment envelope. The fortress's massive black iron cannons aimed seaward. Next stop, The Shot Tower where soldiers at the top poured molten lead to the ground, forming bullets for their flintlocks. When the film reel I watched was over, it leaves me thinking of this kind, caring, man, so dominant in our lives. We adored him. I can still smell the old spice shaving lotion he wore as I hugged him.

Every Sunday, Popie and Nannan, the name we called his wife, our grandmother, came to dinner, Steve and I were always over excited. Before dinner, Popie took Steve and I on a new adventure, Duck Pin bowling, the ball small enough for us to hold and roll down the alley.

Nannan was a piano player. She was teaching Steve how to play. Popie, an electrical engineer at Bell Telephone, was keen on my interest in electronics and bought me a subscription to a magazine called *Popular Science* filled with experiments you could do at home. Together we did the one that piqued our interest.

Popie and Nannan still came to Sunday dinner after we moved into a bigger house in the more affluent, ever expanding Baltimore suburbs. Now sixteen and seventeen, Steve's and my weekend social life got busy. We started a rock and roll band, but still made Sunday dinner, playing catch with Popie in the back yard, then dashing off to band practice. I was in love with our singer, Marna Goldman. She had a unique vocal style and classy stage presence. Unfortunately, her family moved to Connecticut. Steve cared nothing about my broken heart. We needed a new singer, period.

A friend of a friend told us about a guy vocalist looking for a gig. We invited him to hear us play. His name was Lucius Barns, and he was black. His voice blew us away. Lucius was just we needed, soul.

One Sunday dinner, sitting around the table, my father announced that he had sold one of his seafood franchises to a chain of Jewish Delicatessen owners.

Unexpectedly, Popie, sneered, "You sold to Jews! What's next, niggers?."

I felt like I was punched in the stomach. My eyes shifted to Steve. He just lowered his head. Our beloved Popie was an anti-Semitic racist. Mom diplomatically changed the subject, but Sunday dinners would never be the same.

Brotherhood

Driving to Guild Hall, East Hampton cultural center. My play, *Brotherhood,* opening night. Quick stop at the East Hampton post office.

The postal clerk says, "Package, Mr. Benderoth. Heavy sucker."

A damaged, dirty cardboard box thumps on the counter. I scan the address. Campbell's Funeral Home, NYC. freak. My brother Steve's ashes. Perfect timing, bro. Crushing my high…again.

Idolization blinded me to Steve's destructive, competitive, covetous traits, not obvious to me until years of therapy. Steve hit on every girlfriend I ever had, cheated copiously on the love of his life Catlin James. Cat from high school onward.

Forewarned is forearmed. No such luck.

Born eighteen months after me. In geologic time…twins. Inseparable mutual lovefest. Brotherhood. Unbreakable.

We had a glorious childhood. Cops and robbers, cowboys and Indians, summers at our Chesapeake Bay shore home, fanatic rock and rollers, our infamous band through high school, "The Centaurs."

College breaks it up. Steve, drama school, me, pre-med. Both back to Baltimore after graduation, me to teach, Steve scoring promos for a local TV station. Biding time. Bigger goals.

Steve reads a want ad in The Rolling Stone. A New York City band, a record contract, looking for a bass player. A gig in

D.C. Steve auditions, nails it, and heads to NYC following his bliss.

Phone call. Cat gleefully pipes, "Let's have a surprise farewell party for Stevie. Just the four of us," meaning Cat, Steve, me and Les." Les...Lesley Parks, my one and only for eight years, now my fiancé.

Cat, bubbly, "I'll decorated your clubroom."

The clubroom. Our notorious den. Wild parties, rock and roll bands, decibels off the charts. Neighborhood menace.

Me, to Cat, "You and Lesley do food, I'll do cocktails."

Cat, overexcited, "Can we have Gimlets, please, my favorite." Gimlets. A deadly concoction of gin, Rose's super sweet lime juice, shaken, not stirred.

The folks escape to the movies. The house is ours. Steve sweetly pretends surprise, brings reefers and cocaine to the mix. Kathy and Lesley adore cocaine as well. Their drug of choice.

Food, mini-Maryland backfin crab cakes, Old Bay steamed shrimp, my contribution, two dozen chilled Chincoteague oysters on the half shell. Aphrodisiacs. Gimlets, coke, grass, oysters, ooh wee, baby! The party begins. Hendrix turned to ten. We laugh and dance the night away.

Too much booze, too many drugs. A careless remark to Lesley. I don't remember what.

Enraged, Lesley runs up the steps, screaming, "All you care about is you, you, you. What about us! What about me! I'm tired of this crap!"

Out the club room door. Slam! Then...THUNDER SLAM!!! Out the front door. Gone. I start after her.

Steve, his palm to my chest, "You're the last person she needs right now. I'll go cool her out, bring her back."

He leaves, I pace.

Steve and Lesley are gone for over an hour. Cat passed out on the couch.

Me, half sober, I check upstairs…no one. Outside. I run up the street to Lesley's house. Locked, lights out, not there. I start back home. It hits. The woods at the bottom of the street. Used to go there to make out. No way. A nauseous wave sweeps. Downhill run slows to a crawl. I hear whispers in the reeds. Nausea displaced by rage.

I scream, "I know you're in there!"

Steve, too coolly, "Give us a minute."

The "us" pierces. A knife in the heart.

Steve's silhouette appears in the rushes. He buttons his shirt, brushes off, strolls out past me. No eye contact. No words. He casually saunters up the hill. Blasé. So—him.

Lesley's shadowy, rumpled image fights the reeds. Peers in my eyes, "He didn't make me pregnant."

She wobbles. I try to steady. "Don't touch me," she scowls. "It was all your fault…and don't follow me."

She dissolves in the night. My legs don't work, not booze, stupor. I break free. Walk home. I crash. Comatose.

Next morning, hung over, the wordless drive to Penn Station for the New York train. Steve riding shotgun like I am not there. I park. He gets out, casually grabs his bag, jaunts to the platform. Escape? I can't. Not yet. I stay. I watch. Train arrives. Steve hops on. Departs. Gone. Brotherly love, lost. Brotherhood, lost.

Years fly with Steve a top TV jingle writer in New York, me, a Hollywood screenwriter.

Alex, Steve's daughter, my niece, calls frantically…too often, spilling Steve's blitz into drugs and booze.

"Detox again…" or "Dad and Mom separated…" or "They got a divorce."

Steve spirals deeper, deeper, deeper.

Therapists warn me away. It sucks you in. Enough on your plate. I do. My wife Nancy is bedridden. A brain tumor. I'm her caregiver. My sanctuary, a playwright's group. We read our work aloud, offer positive feedback. One play is selected at the end of each season for a staged reading. New York actors, scripts in hand, sitting on stage or walking through the play with a skeletal set and props. My play *Brotherhood* is chosen. Ecstatic.

Ecstasy is shattered by him again. After years of cold silence, Steve calls. "Hey Mick."

Me, queasy, "Been a while."

Him, too friendly, "Two-way street, bro."

Dead airtime.

"Whatever," he quips.

Me, blasé, his style, "So, what's been hapnin' bro?"

"You know damn well what's happening. Alex called you."

I said, "Yeah, she told me. You're on dialysis. Seven days a week.

Steve, "It's hell on earth. So, I bailed."

"Bailed? You'll die."

"Not if I get a kidney transplant. Listen Mick, I've never asked you for anything"

No, he never asked. He just took.

Steve sounds frantic, "My life's on the line."

Me, "I can't help you, Steve."

Steve, bitterly, "Can't or won't."

"Can't."

"You're my brother. Blood."

"I've had hepatitis. Years ago. You remember. Gamma globulin shots. I can't give blood, I can't donate."

"Bullshit."

"So be it."

"Whatever." Click.

Delirious that my play was chosen, I go all the way. A set designer friend is dressing the stage. I work with my dream cast every day. Hard. I'm in heaven. Play rehearsal.

Stagehand, "Phone call Mick."

Must be Nancy, I say to myself.

On the phone, "Hello."

"Mick Benderoth?"

"Yes."

"Sergeant Winbourn, NYPD."

The police? What the hell? "Yes, officer, how can I help you?"

"I'm sorry to report that your brother Steven Carl Benderoth died. Cleaning woman found him in bed."

Horrifying image. Instant impulse. "I'll take care of funeral arrangements."

"The body will be at the morgue."

Morgue. My brother, toe tagged, in a morgue fridge. Stultifying.

Winbourn, "The funeral home can pick it up there."

"It." …My brother an "It."

Winbourn, "Sorry for your loss."

"Thank you." Click.

Parked outside Guild Hall, Steve's ashes shock me, aggressively commanding, "I wanna come into the theater."

Me, queasy, wary, "I don't feel…"

"Screw your feelings. Gotta see my story on stage." Ego still blazing.

Me, "Our story."

"Whatever."

His ashes under my arm, I go apprehensively into the theater.

Curtain.

Brotherhood is well received, but my brother, Steve, screwed me again. From the grave. Even in death, his ashes killed my glory.

Brotherhood, dead and buried.

What's in a Name?

Nancy Perl my wife of forty-six years, is a woman of many names. Her grandparents on her mother's side are Russian Jews, the Whittners. They have two daughters, Annabel, and Edna. Annabel and Edna change their name from Whittner to Whitney, think it sounds more American. Annabel and Edna, The Whitney Sisters, become Ziegfeld Follies girls.

Nancy's paternal great grandparents, Jews from Poland, Menzer and Blume Israel. Menzer changes his name from Israel to Reals, for obvious reasons. Annabel Whitney meets Barney Reals, they have a son Martin Reals and daughter Nancy Ann Reals.

Nancy, a precocious, gifted painter moves to Manhattan, goes to Pratt and the Art Students League, and thrives, but she has to pay the rent. Nancy lands a job as an assistant in an off-off Broadway show in production, "The World of Sholom Aleichem," produced by a McCarthy blacklisted playwright, Arnold Perl. The costume designer's looking for an assistant. Nancy's portfolio gets her the job.

By the end of the run, Nancy, nineteen, was dating Arnold Perl, forty. Nancy married Arnold a year later. Nancy Ann Reals Perl.

Nancy keeps her professional name Nancy Reals until she doesn't. She's working in Paris, Arnold tries in vain to locate her. Her hotel has no Nancy Perl registered. After heated dickering–Arnold is quick to dicker–he locates Nancy, registered as Nancy Reals. Angry, Arnold could get angry.

Reason, ego, Arnold has a big one. Nancy didn't use her married name, Nancy Perl, to sign in. Nancy a quick study learns. Now, Nancy Ann Reals Perl.

Eighteen years later, making a documentary about Malcolm X, Arnold fifty-seven, has a massive heart attack fixing breakfast for his two little girls Becky and Sarah. Nancy is a widow at thirty-six.

This is where I come in. I'm editing the film. Nancy and I are called to Hollywood to finish the documentary, a year later we're lovers. I move in with Nancy and her girls. We finally marry. Nancy is now Nancy Ann Reals Perl Benderoth. Nancy still uses her professional name, Nancy Reals Perl. I never, ever hear her use our married name, Nancy Benderoth. I understand, sort of.

Nancy turns fifty. Bad news. Breast cancer. She recovers but is beset by a series of medical maladies and finally, a brain disease. Bed ridden for years, with me her sole care provider, watching the love of my life wither away.

Nancy talks less and less. We play a game every morning, me bedside, "Sweetheart, what's my name?"

She searches, finally, "Mick Benderoth."

Me again, "And what's your name?"

Short silence., yet again, "Nancy Reals Perl."

Near the end, she can hardly speak. Three days before her death, I try to play our name game for the last time.

"What's my name, darling?"

Her eyes dim, watery, nothing.

"Honey, what's your name?" Constant eye contact.

Nancy pauses, then a wispy, "Nancy Benderoth." The last words she ever says. Nancy Benderoth, my companion, partner, and lover.

What's in a name? Love, love is in a name. My wife, woman of many names. Nancy Ann Reals Perl Benderoth.

Her final gift. The name I longed to hear, Nancy Benderoth

Writing on
the Wall

Steve hummed imperceptibly, constantly from day one. I never recognized any of it, but was always there…Steve's music, I came to think of it as his head hums.

He taught himself piano at eight, clearly playing head hums, original tunes.

I can't carry one, but rhythm, I had. I was nine, saved up twenty-five cents a week, bought a pair of drumsticks, tapping in time to Dorsey Brother's classics, from my dad's 78 rpm collection.

Bam! The Fifties. Dorsey's are history. Here comes Elvis…The King. Steve copies his hair, collar way up, buys an acoustic guitar from Sears with twenty dollars of birthday money, learns every "Hound Dog" chord in a week.

My move, a well-worn, third-hand snare drum, replete with aged, dented brass cymbal, a pawn shop prize.

Steve strumming, gyrating, me beating skins. Guitar and drums. Band number one.

Crash! "The Sixties," now band number five… "he Centaurs. Steve powers up to a Fender electric bass, amp up to his shoulders. Warning. Do not stand in front of the cabinet. My ears are still ringing.

Me, full Gretsch kit, Zildjian cymbals, over the top. Tommy Blake, our lead guitarist, Elgin Jones, our, savvy Black singer, seduced from a rival band. Kick ass, R&R covers, no band played originals. Kids wanted what they wanted. AM radio. Period.

During college, the band scatters. Steve, to Carnegie Tech. Me, to University of Maryland. Four years fly, we graduate into Vietnam, the war, the draft. I teach, an automatic deferment. Steve charms some lady shrink. Diagnosis. Homosexual. Steve…4-F.

Steve eyes a want ad in Rolling Stone. A New York City rock band, The Hangmen, landed an ABC record contract, looking for a bass player. Steve trains to New York for an audition. He plays. Off the charts. The new bass man for The Hangmen.

The band, Tony Taylor, sexy, strong vocalist. George Strunz, classic flamenco roots, turned rock lead guitarist. Ritchie Blakin, flashy, powerful jazz drummer, now rock. Rhythm guitar, Jon St. John. Steve Benderoth, thumping bass.

Problem one. ABC thinks the band's name sucks. The Hangmen brainstorm. Steve throws out a new buzz word. Graffiti, Writing on the Wall. It sticks.

Problem two. The band has no original music. ABC is putting on the pressure. Where's the fucking album?

Steve's humming. His time. Confidently, he announces, "I'll write it."

Sequestered in a shabby room at New York's infamous Hotel Albert, Steve emerges with twelve songs in hand, enough for an album. Graffiti lays it all down.

Serendipity. Eddie Kramer, famed recording engineer to Jimi Hendrix, Woodstock, Crosby, Stills and Nash, and Joni Mitchell, is in town between gigs and owes ABC a favor.

Steve's music, Kramer's genius produces an album beyond expectations. Review copies, kudos, "A progressive psychedelic ensemble blending progressive rock, jazz, classical, R&B with unique multi-level harmonies. A sure-fire hit"

ABC is ecstatic. Get this band on the road. Promote the hell out of it.

Steve sends me the album, Special Delivery. Beyond entranced, I replay it for hours. Steve's humming on vinyl forever.

Side bar 1: Ambiguous serendipity. Steve's college roommate, Bob Boris, a copy writer with BBD&O primo ad agency, Bob's account, Pepsi, new product, Scandi, a berry flavored soda. Top echelon jingle writers vie for the prize. Residuals. Big money. Boris fenagles Steve and the band into the mix.

Steve sequesters, re-surfaces, Graffiti nails it. Boris submits, Pepsi "Yes!"

A fly in Steve's ointment. Coca Cola beats out Pepsi, releasing Cherry Coke first. Scandi…bagged. Band blows it off.

Side bar 2: Top music house MZH, producers of Scandi jingle, sense Steve's promise as a TV commercial jingle writer Opens their door. Steve files it away. Graffiti priority one.

Squash. Another humongous fly. Graffiti's manager skips with ABC's advance money, contract broken.

Hoping to recoup, ABC releases the album. No fanfare. No tour. The kiss of death. The album is remaindered, and Graffiti is history. The band crumbles. Lead singer Taylor desperately tries to hold it all together. Strunz splits, back to flamenco, St. John to brother's band in L.A.

Taylor and drummer Blakin plead with Steve. We can do it again. Steve's dream meets a fork in the road. Faces the dilemma, Graffiti or MZH offer of fame and fortune. Seduced. Steve walks through the door,

Taylor harshly, "Sellout!" They never speak again.

A deal with the devil? Humming in his head becomes jingles on the tube.

One year, Steve's MZH hot, new jingle man, in demand. Stellar client list, General Mills, Procter & Gamble, Seven Up, Bounty paper toweling, "Bounty, the quicker picker upper," runs for years. King of the jingle for twenty-five years.

215

Over the years he starts to slow down, slower, slower. Stops cold. Never writes another song. After a harrowing battle with drugs and alcohol, he suffers kidney failure, no transplants in sight due to his continued drinking and declining health. His fight to continue living depended on arduous, stressful dialysis treatments. He makes the descension to stop dialysis, a sure death sentence, in essence he is committing suicide.

He passes painfully in 2010.

A self-destructing talent is a human tragedy. Spurning artistic glory for financial gain and adulation is evidence of a lack of character. Yet it was compounded by his heinous behavior toward friends and loved ones. These combined were the devil's paybacks. Steven Carl Benderoth's Faustian legacy.

Advice

Lizzie McKenzie, it has a nice ring to it. Lizzy and I went to Miller High School, but she was way out of my league. Tall, blond, blue eyes, and a smile to die for, Lizzy McKenzie a senior, me, a lowly sophomore. She held the school in the palm of her hand. President of the Student Council, and her crowning glory, editor of the school newspaper, which is where we became friends, me a cub reporter, covering what she threw my way. Under her creative guidance, *Millers Monthly* was regarded as the top school paper in Baltimore.

After high school, Lizzy went to journalism school at Columbia. I went to a small college for pre-med, to please my mother. My dream of Hollywood, impossible for her to comprehend. Disregarding my parents' atavistic desires, I achieved my dream, gloriously becoming a Hollywood screenwriter for fifteen years. Heaven.

One dream realized; another begins. I return to New York, starting a TV commercial production company with my wife, Nancy. She produced, I directed, heaven again. Two dreams belted, yearning for more. A heartbreaking tragedy thwarted my dream path. Nancy died after a long brain illness. I was her sole caregiver. Devastated, I found sanctuary in our East Hampton home. to heal, recover from the trauma of losing the love of my life.

Lizzy returned to Baltimore when *The Evening Sun,* the city's main rag, hired her to write an advice column, by-line,

"Listen to Lizzy." Quite a coup for a twenty-one-year-old journalism grad.

I found that I could grieve and work together. I took freelance directing work. My skill was remembered. Clients old and new wanted me. I zenithed, shooting classics for Pepsi, IBM, Jaguar, and American Airlines,

But caring for Nancy had wearied me. It resurfaced. I fell into a deep depression. Grieving is a complex process. I lost my bearings, a little boy in the center of an infinite field of grass having no idea which way to turn, one of the children Holden Caufield dreamed of saving. I was unsalvageable. Years of intense talk and group therapy helped but did little to re-socialize me. I just wanted to be alone. I couldn't read or write, see a movie or watch TV. I was stuck.

Then one morning, out of more boredom, I picked up *The Times* in my apartment building lobby. Half-heartedly flipping pages, I saw her picture, her name, Lizzy Mackenzie, byline "Listen to Lizzy." She achieved her goal, advice columnist for the *New York Times.*

I was stunned, intrigued and desperate, desperate enough to reach out to an advice columnist for help? A woman I went to high school with? Ridiculous, but I'm at my wit's end. I need some advice.

Sitting at my computer in a cold sweat, I type one word: lonely. I feel like a fool, but automatically press send. Instantly I regret it. Why did I stoop to this? I must really be losing it. I put the whole demeaning blunder out of my head, continuing to hide in the sanctuary of my apartment.

One day, checking my cell for missed calls, which I instantly delete, I see a number from *The New York Times.* "I freeze, motionless, paralyzed, then a me I do not know steps up and dials the number. A young, cheery voice answers, "Lizzy Mackenzie's office." My mouth, the Gobi Desert, my mind, blank. Say something idiot.

"Rick Learner returning your call."

"Oh, Mr. Learner, Lizzy's been hoping you'd call back. I'll put you through." PING!

"Well, well, well, Mick Benderoth, it's been a while. So, we both wound up in New York City. Doo ya miss ol' Bal-more, hon?," She speaks in the unmistakable Baltimore dialect.

I play back on autopilot, "I liv donna street, hon, cross frum at Linkin Cener thing, eva seen it?"

"Bin air a while ago, think I saw some kinda music, or sumthin," she beams.

Reality kicks in. "Mick Benderoth, I saw your email, and tracked you down. How are you doing? What are you doing? What have you been doing? It's been forty years, and you come to your old high school boss for advice. What did you write...lonely?"

"Yes," I answered drawing out the word.

"Meaning what exactly?," she questions politely.

"A long, long, saga," I answer.

"Well, we all have one, don't we? Seems like we have a hell of a lot of catching up to do. Lunch! Tomorrow! I'll clear my schedule."

Lunch? Tomorrow? I hadn't seen anyone except my doorman in months. Get a grip asshole.

"I'd love to," I blurt out.

"1:30 at Gallagher's, they grill a mean burger, onion rings to die for, all right by you?"

"Sure," I force out.

"Fabulous, we'll yak till they close the place. I'm so excited. See you tomorrow."

"Bye hon," she giggles. "Lookin ford to it an all,"

I 'Bal-more' back.

I set my cell alarm, take a melatonin, turn on a "Star Trek" episode I'd seen a thousand times, plop onto my pillow, eyes wide open, unable to relax, no trace of sleep in my brain. Just what I need, an all-nighter. Fate was kind. I conk.

Waking in a mindless daze, it hits me, lunch. Lizzy Mackenzie. I bolt, shower, shave, facing the usual stranger in the mirror, a seventy-year-old caricature of me. My grey-white beard needs a trim, my hair, whatever was left, hangs down to my shoulders. Gotta go with what you got.

What to wear? Sweatpants and tee shirts, my daily attire, left me clueless. I open the closet, grab a silk shirt, still in the dry cleaner's plastic sheath, a pair of new black Levi's, tags dangling, and socks, no longer an accessory.

Dressed way early, I drift into the kitchen, no coffee, jumpy enough already. I sit at my computer to finish a scene in a play I was writing, blocked for months. Time passes. My cell alarm scares me.

I cab to Gallagher's, amble to the podium where a quirky, petite young woman blinks at me.

"Can I…?"

A voice chimes out. "Ova heer, Hun! I got us a spot with an umbrella!" There she is! Lizzy Mackenzie, standing like a beacon, beckoning me to the table. Hair no longer blond and flowing, but bright white, clipped short, like Twiggy, if you can remember back that far, breathtaking.

Weaving through the diners, she rushes up and gives me a super hug. A whiff of her subtle, so Lizzy perfume, makes me dizzy, a teenager on his first date.

"Oh, Mick, my dear, dear friend."

My eyes tear up. She gently, slips out of the hug, eyes teary as well, kisses me on both cheeks. I kiss back. She tastes like…like Lizzy.

We sit. She pulls a monogrammed hanky from her purse, leans across the table, and blots my eyes, then her own.

A waiter shuffles up to our table. "Anything to drink?"

"Two infinitely dry Safire Blue Martinis, onions…you?," flashing those big blues at me.

"The same."

"Arctic frigid," she orders. "Be right back," grins the waiter.

"So, let's cut to the chase. Lonely means what?" I take a deep breath, I start, "My wife died three years ago."

Lizzy reaches across the table and caresses my cheek. "I'm so, so sorry, Mick. How long were you together?"

"Forty-six years, half fantastic, half rough. It's...I don't really have words, watching...watching..."

"I know. I lost my only child, my twelve-year old son, Anthony, twenty years ago...leukemia. Torture, exhaustion, heartbreak, alone. I divorced his father years ago. He lives in California. Visited when he wasn't—too busy," she says sharply.

The waiter brings our drinks. "Let's toast to...?"

"Ann...Ann Winthrop Learner," I softly reply.

"And to Anthony Mackenzie Warren," she adds smiling. "And to us," she says defiantly.

We raise, clink and sip. The gin warms me up. I relax, we exchange personal histories for hours, never get around to ordering.

Her cell rings. She answers. "Oh, yes. I'm running late, cover for me." She smiles at me. "I have to get back for a meeting. Come with me. I'll drop you off."

I pay the check, haphazardly tossing a handful of twenties on the table and follow her.

She steps into the street, puts two fingers in her mouth and whistles! Lizzy Mackenzie, Whistles...like an umpire. Two cabs screech over. She opens the door of the closest one, waves bye-bye to the other.

Getting into the cab, she scoots over, flashing those eyes again, "We can discuss dinner plans on our way, Awlrite, Hon?."

"Awlrite! Yeah, awlrite! The best damn advice, I've gotten in years, hon!"

Bliss

Cooking was my bliss. I say "was" because now that I live alone—my wife passed three years ago—I grab a yogurt from the fridge, or slap together a PB&J. I eat standing up.

As a child, I stood beside my grandmother as she cooked for our family in a tiny kitchen on an ancient porcelain gas stove. Aromas from bubbling, sizzling pots and pans enveloped the room. My sanctuary.

Grandma cooked what she knew, drawing from her German heritage. Fluffy dumplings, dressed in fried onions and bacon, golden schnitzel, topped with a fried egg, savory sauerbraten. Heaven.

Being Marylanders, we also feasted on the bounty from the Chesapeake Bay. Oysters any way, on the half shell, coated with cracker crumbs and deep fried, crispy on the outside, savory juicy oysters inside. Oyster stew, a milk and cream broth, barely simmering, raw oysters dropped in at the last minute, served immediately, and the renowned Maryland crab cake, a Friday night treat.

I mastered this cuisine when my father impulsively bought Sterling's Seafood, a tiny shop on the corner. The family legend goes that Sterling, a man in his late seventies, once shouted to his devoted customers, "Fifty years is long enough, I'd sell this damn place for a dime."

Joking, my father, Ben, pulled a dime from his pocket and slapped it on the counter.

Sterling shouted, "Ben is the new owner of Sterling's seafood."

My father built Sterling's into a thriving franchise, branches extending into the newly developing Baltimore suburbs.

I earned my stripes working every summer in the kitchen. Apprentice, sous chef, to cook.

My father, chuckled, "Keep this up, Mick, and someday you'll own this place."

Cooking, divine, running a restaurant, no way. My father seldom came home.

I took my zeal to college, paying my way with a part time job at a French bistro, Claudette's. I swept, washed, shopped, and chopped. Cleaning the counter one night, I spotted a food-stained cookbook. Some woman named Julia Childs.

"Take it," Claudette said. "Learn." I did, reveling in feeding family and friends for half a century.

Fifty years later, I stand with an empty peanut butter jar in my hand. The fridge empty, save for a bowl of cooked spinach, age unknown, a jar with four shriveled black olives, in the crisper, one floppy scallion, a potato so sprouted it looked like an octopus, and God knows why, a petrified clove of garlic stuck in the corner. The freezer, gruesome. Two Swanson dinners with a freezer-burned chicken breast wedged between them. Take out? Again? What has happened to me? Who am I? Am I dead? Is this hell? I will not go down like this.

I whipped out a dish towel, tucked it under my belt.

I thawed the chicken breast in a bowl of cool water, peeled, and julienned the potato, soaking the match sticks in ice water to crisp. I pounded the chicken breast between layers of a garbage bag.

Drained and dried, the spuds were tossed in a hot pot with an inch of olive, the chicken in a frying pan. Minced, the olives, garlic, and scallions, were spooned into a coffee cup, with a last part of ancient butter, nuked for two minutes. Sizzling!

Bubbling! Aromas! Aromas! It's me! I'm alive! I'm back! Plated, the sautéed chicken, glistening with olive, scallion, and garlic, perfect pomme frites, buttered spinach my side dish.

I sat down at my marble cafe table, a white cloth napkin on my lap and felt whole, as Julia's spirit sang out, "Bon Appetite!." Bliss

Tres J's

John Joseph Jenkins, nickname "J," was a good friend of mine. He was an icon, the epitome of a troubadour, aging gracefully. Long white hair, well-trimmed white beard, wearing a well-worn tee shirt, a picture of Hendrix on the front, the word "Experience" on the back. Old jeans, old holes ripped in the knees. Wore a huge silver and Onyx ring, a silver "J" on the stone.

A classically trained flamenco guitarist, who'd played on many of my brother Steve's TV commercial jingles. He could sight read, play any style or genre needed to get the job done. Made his living as a coveted session guitarist, but a flamenco man at heart. We often jammed together, then cooled out, sitting around, smoking a joint, passing a bottle of Maduro Tequila. J was a natural raconteur. Been there and then some. He started into one of his tales. We were mesmerized. As usual. This time he blew us away.

I'm deep in a groove. Knock at the door. Don't hear it. Louder knocks. Oblivious. Still grooving.

A young male voice screams while fist pounds. "Open the door! Open the fuckin door! Got your damn groceries!"

I finally hear the yelling. Snap out of the groove. Saunter to the door. Opens it. A Hispanic boy about twelve stands with two scrunched grocery bags held awkwardly by one arm. Free arm, pounder.

"Banging for ten minutes. I ain't got all day, Old Man."

"Sorry. Didn't hear ya."

"You deaf?"

"Not yet. Put the bags on the kitchen floor. Who are you anyway? Where's Santos?"

"On vacation. He's my bro. Filling in."

"Vacation, hell. Busted dealing H."

"Where'd you hear that?"

"Miguel, when I gave him my order."

"Fuckin' bigmouth."

"Doing time?"

"Whatta you care."

"I like him."

"Already sprung."

"Who paid?"

"Friends with money."

"Friends? I bet.

Boy smirks.

J, "Put the bags on the kitchen floor."

The boy sets them down. Starts out.

"Pay you if you unpack."

"How much?"

"You tell me."

"Five bucks"

"Five it is."

Boy starts unpacking. "Where's this stuff go?"

"Cold, the fridge. Rest, closets."

Kid spots J's. ring. "Cool finger bling. What's the "J" stand for?"

"For "J." My name."

"I'm J too. Jose. Two J's."

J, "How about that."

Boy, "I'm done. Pay up. If I'm late Manuel will can my ass."

J hands Jose a bill.

"That's a ten."

"You earned it.

"Santos said you tipped big. Thanks."

"You're welcome."

Days later, I'm making breakfast. Doorbell. Damn. Turn off the gas, answer the door. It's Jose with bags.

Jose, holds his nose "What's stinks?"

J, "Making Huevos Rancheros."

Jose puts down the grocery bags and strides into the kitchen.

"Hey old man that's not how you make Huevos Rancheros. Sit down and let someone who knows what they're doing take over."

As I scrape my disaster into garbage, Jose takes command. Finishes.

J, "You aced it, Jose. Best damn Rancheros I ever, ever had. Thanks compadre."

Jose, "You want Mexican, you call be." Writes his phone number on the kitchen wall.

I smile broadly. Jose opens the door to leave. Turns back.

Joe, "Hey, J. You know the lady in 30D?"

"No. Keep to myself."

"She plays music too. Piano. Old stuff. Some guy Mote something."

"Mozart."

"Oughta check her out."

"Mind your business. *Vete muchacho.*"

"You speak Spanish?"

"Enough to get you moving."

Jose, smiles, "See ya round …J."

I grin, "Back at cha …J."

I step out of the shower. Towel wrapped. Doorbell rings. Call out, "Just a minute." Throw on my robe. Go to the door.

A woman, gray hair, fashionable bob, very attractive. "Oh my, looks like I caught you at a bad time."

"Perfectly alright. Can I help you?"

"I'm Janet Winthrop, 30 B. Jose, the delivery boy said you were a musician. That I should, how did he say it, check you out."

"Oh, he did, did he?"

"Not so?"

"No matter. I'm John Jenkins. Call me 'J.'"

"I'm Janice. Jan."

"Another J."

"Pardon?"

"Inside joke. Come on in, sit while I change."

"Actually, I came to ask if you'd like to come to our music club tomorrow afternoon. All friends. All musicians. We play and chat."

J, hesitant, "I don't know."

"Jose says you're a guitarist."

"I play some."

"Bring it along."

"Not sure I can make it."

Jan, sweetly persistent, "Other plans?"

"Well, no, but…"

"We meet at three. Good for you?"

"Well, ah…"

"Till then…J." Spins around. Leaves. Door closed.

J, "Damn little devil."

At the music club, a grand piano commands the room. Eight people sit chatting. The doorbell rings. Jan opens the door to see me in my one white shirt, black necktie, sport coat, unholey jeans. Natty. Guitar case in my hand.

Jan's cordial, "Well, you made it." She turns and faces the group. "People, we have a new member today. This is "J," A guitarist." They all nod and smile.

Jan, To J, "Come in. Have some wine. Red or white?"

J, "Red."

She hands him a glass of wine, "We usually ask new members to play first. Is that alright with you, J?"

"Well," taking my guitar from its case, "I don't have anything prepared," To Jan, "You by chance know Vivaldi's 'Concerto in D?'"

Jan, surprised, "I'll pull the score up on my tablet. Got it."

Jan starts. She's good. I drift in. Slide into her groove Piano and guitar, a perfect duet. The room's enchanted. Jan keeps looking over at me, enthralled. Jump back in again, way deep in the groove. The piece ends. Jan nods to me. Well, I nod back.

We stand up, side by side, humorously bow in sync.. The group titters, stands, applauds. A few bravos thrown in. They gather around me. Many kudos. An hour of chit chat follows. I get that feeling. I'm a bit out of place. Jan sees me. Catches my drift Winks. Looks at her watch.

"Oh my. Time to close." People depart shaking hands with J. Jan takes him by the arm, beams,

"I had no idea. Jose said…"

"Rock and roll."

"Yes, but..."

"Juilliard. Unfortunately, rock pays better than classical." J gently glides his hand over the piano top. "Bösendorfer. Vienna. Very fine."

"You know your stuff. It's a gift from my late husband." We walk to the door. Jan says, "Next week?"

"Have to see. Thanks for the invite. Enjoyed it."

"I'm glad. Nice to have a friend on the same floor. Bye, J."

I leave. Walk to my place with jaunty gate, talking to his guitar. "We did good, ol' buddy, really good."

I'm vacuuming. Hair in a ponytail, bandana around my head. Loud door knock. Yell. "Hey J, It's me! Jose. Got your stuff."

Turn off vacuum, open the door. Fist bump.

"You pulled a fast one on me…J. Mrs. Winthrop."

"Said you was great." Sets down groceries. Starts putting them away.

"Still covering for Santos?"

"Ain't seen him. Layin' low. You always clean your place?"

"Exercise."

"Mom's a cleaner. Cheap. You could get her. I'll text you her number."

"I do just fine."

"She could use the money."

"Text me. Your father?"

"Died. Never knew him. Sisters never knew theirs either. Santiago's father was bad. Shot in a gangbang. J...? I'm gonna be sixteen Friday. Having a party. I was hoping you could come."

"Not a party guy."

"Mrs. Winthrop's coming. You don't need to bring no present or nothing. Maybe your guitar."

I grin, "Hiring me to entertain?"

"Come. Please. A favor. I'll pick you guys up."

Jose finishes the groceries. I reach for my wallet.

"On me. Now you owe me one. My party."

"Guess you got me." Fist bump. Jose leaves. I go back to vacuuming.

Friday. Doorbell. Jan and Jose. Jan, "I'm here with our escort."

On the street. I hail a cab.

Jose asks, "A cab?"

"Special occasion." Open the door for Jan "Why thank you kind sir." She slides in. Jose pauses, warily.

J, "You gonna gawk all day?

Jose, "Never been in one before. Somebody sees me, never live it down."

"Get in. My present."

"Thanks...I guess."

Cab pulls up to a project building. Jan and I get out. Jose, "Have to walk around to the front." We follow Jose. Out of nowhere! Santos, heavy breathing, dripping sweat. Terrified. Jose, "What's going down, bro.?"

Gun shots. Close. Loud. Down the street. Black car driving fast. Shooter, out the window. BLAM! BLAM! Santo's splits around the corner. Jose pushes me and Jan to the ground. Jumps on top, covering them. More shots. BLAM! BLAM! Car drives by, squeals around the corner. More shots. Silence. Jose gets to his feet to help Jan up. "You all OK.?"

"I'm ok."

Me to Jose, "You?" Jose holds up bloody hands. "I...I dunno...I...I..." Knees buckle. I catch him. Lowers him to the ground. Jan, cell in hand, calls 911. Jose, losing it. Murmurs. "But It's my birthday."

"Hold on, J...hold on. Helps coming."

Jose, "My party...my party."

"We're here, buddy. Were right here." Jose stops breathing. "Oh, Jesus God no...no." Jan kneels close, tear streaked. "EMS is on the way."

I bust out crying, rocking Jose in his arms. "He's...gone, Jan. He's gone."

Me and Jan paused inside the funeral home at Jose's casket. I say, "Life owed you so much more, you gave me so much."

Take off my ring, gently put it on Jose's finger. Jan bends in. Kisses Jose lightly on the cheek. Me and Jan walk down the aisle to the door. I take Jan's hand. We hold the third "J" in their hearts, forever.

Sunshine

"You are my sunshine,
My only sunshine,
You make me happy
When skies are grey
You'll never know dear
How much I love you
Please don't take
My sunshine away."

"Thanks, Poppop that's my favorite."
"Mine too."
"You can tuck me in."
"How's that?"
"Good, I can go to sleep now."
"Nighty night, Baby Boy."

I'd been taking care of my grandson, Griffin, for several months. Griff was really my step grandson. His real one, died long before he was born. Rebecca put Griff in my arms when he was thirteen days old. Eye contact. Bonded immediately. Joined at the heart from that day forward.

I was fifty, he was five. His parents, my stepdaughter Rebecca and her husband Tom, had gone to Omaha. Rebecca needed a T-Cell transplant for the non-Hodgkin's lymphoma. I never had children of my own, so taking care of Griff was the closest I ever came to fatherhood.

My wife, Nancy, thirteen years my senior, was not well, bedridden. So, Griff was my sole responsibility. Griffin often took snacks to Nancy. She would read him a story while they munched on Hershey's Kisses. They were soulmates.

Griff and I did everything together, jumping the shallow waves at the beach, shopping at local farm stands, ice cream at Carvel's, running through the lawn sprinkler, swimming in the pool. We were active from morning till night, when I put him to bed, and sang him to sleep. I was exhausted at first, but actually got in better shape. I loved it, and adored Griff.

I was now seventy-five and living alone. Taking care of the house was more than I expected. I hired most of the work out, but the bottom step of the front door was rotten and I feared tripping. I took on the task.

"Goddamn back," I yelped, trying to pick up a wood plank.

"Poppop!" Griff's strong voice lifted my spirits.

"Baby Boy. Just in time."

He leaned his bike against a willow tree, the ever-present guitar case slung on his back. His rock band rented a place up the road for the summer. They were playing at a local bar.

"You could fall again, Poppop. You want to wear a cast for another ten weeks," he warned.

"I wanted to do something myself for a change. Taking care of this place used to be easy, now my body says otherwise," I grumbled.

"No sweat," he said, as he laid the new step in place.

"How's the music going? "I asked.

"Had a full house last night. Jacob extended the gig through August."

"How's old Jake doing? He made a mean margarita."

"It was his son, Poppop, Mr. Jacobs died last year. You were at the wake, remember."

"Oh, right, you let me sit in on bass. I still had my chops then," I said.

"You still do. I love the lyrics you emailed me about Grandma. They remind me of how much I miss her. Did you write the music yet?"

"My hands are too stiff to play. Guess it will have to be a poem," I sighed.

"I'll write the music for it." Griffin spent five years at the Oberlin getting a master's in music composition. "That's a lot to ask. I know you're busy."

"I want to. We can co-write it."

"Your Grandma would have loved that. Will you sing it too? "I beamed.

"Absolutely."

We turned to the task at hand. "Where are the nails?" Griff asked, picking up my hammer.

"Nails, right, the nails." I checked my pockets. "Guess I left them in the cellar. I'll get them."

"I'll get them. You sit. I'll be right back." I watched him vault up the steps, onto the porch and into the house. A man now, where did the 25 years go? I still hear myself singing him to sleep. Griff came out carrying two frosty bottles of beer. He handed me one.

"Here's to us," he toasted.

"You bet Baby Boy." We clinked bottles. I drank deep. Delicious. He piped up, "Why don't we talk a walk, stretch our legs." My knees were killing me. I didn't know if I could, but wouldn't say no. We made it to the beach. A breeze brought the smell of the sea. A redolence reminding me of my wife. She had gone swimming every day.

I winced as I sat down on the hot sand. The surf was rough. Magnificent. "Want to walk down to the water?" Griff asked.

"You'll have to help me get up." Griff grabbed my arms. I struggled to stand, but I made it. Impulsively, I pulled him to my chest and gave him a deep hug.

"Baby Boy, I don't know what I'd do without you. I love you more than I can say."

"I know Poppop, I know."

I kissed him on his cheek and gave him another squeeze. We broke the hug, I took off my docksiders, Griff took my arm, and we headed to the water.

My leg buckled and I went down on one knee.

"You ok?" Griff asked. "You want to walk back?"

"Not when we've gotten this far." Water covered my feet. I used to swim in the ocean this cold. How long ago was that? How long ago?

"Ready to head back?" Griff asked. "Here, I'll hold your arm." His grip felt reassuring. By the time we got home I was played out.

"Help me up the steps, Baby Boy. Think I'm going to sit for a while," I said, breathlessly.

He supported me as I started up. The new step felt safer. I walked to the porch and plopped into the rocking chair that had belonged to my wife's father. "Why don't you play something." I asked.

Griff smiled, taking his guitar out of the case, tuning it, strumming a few chords.

"What's it going to be, Baby Boy?"

"Just close your eyes and relax," he sweetly whispered.

I did what my grandson told me as he started singing.

"You are my sunshine,
My only sunshine,
You make me happy
When skies are grey
You'll never know dear
How much I love you
Please don't take
My sunshine away."

I was fast asleep.

Epilogue

Give-back time. Here's some stuff I've learned from fifty years in film to keep ya'll hangin' in, en' keepin' on truckin', aware of pitfalls on your journey. Forewarned is forearmed.

The ember in my belly started sizzilin' when I saw the original Universal classics, *Frankenstein* and *The Wolfman,* a double feature at our local movie theater. Movies. I had to make them. Belly fire set ablaze on my tenth Birthday when Kodak's first 8 mm home movie camera was placed in my hands. I shiver. A gift from the movie Gods. I was a filmmaker.

My first short films started as scribbles on pieces of paper. Then rough sketches of each scene, storyboarding. Soon I was faced with *screenwriting.* Formatting a screenplay can be learned from any number of help books. Syd Field's classic, *Screenplay: The Foundations of Screenwriting,* is by far the most useful. Syd's cardinal rule, "You must write twenty scripts before you have one that you dare make public."

My journey would not have been possible without meeting movie screenwriting guru's on my way. Waldo Salt, legendary screenwriting pro, taught me a crucial lesson. Waldo wrote the Academy Award Winner, *Midnight Cowboy.* He started writing in the '40's, scads of classics. Google. Waldo's credits will amaze.

After receiving an assignment from 20th Century Fox, where he was a contract writer, Waldo takes a box of typing paper, opens it, puts the empty lid on the right side of his typewriter, the full box on the left. Takes a sheet from left, rolls into the typewriter, writes page one. Done. Puts it face down in the empty top on the right. He never, ever looks back at his day's work till all of paper in the left box is in the right box, now called a *zero draft.*

247

Advice from Waldo: "Don't friggin' touch what you just did. If you dare peek, you are dead in the water. Paralyzed. It will twist and turn you backwards." You'll never even get to draft zero. Waldo then dumps the full box, the zero draft, into the empty box. Now it begins. Rewriting, rewriting, rewriting, till he has his first draft, 'one louda than zero'. Thank you Nigel Tuffnel.

A nugget from my first mentor, Arnold Perl, who wrote the play that produced *Fiddler on the Roof.* "End each workday knowing the next lines you're about to write. Stop! Do not pass go. Then, when you come back to work, you already know what your next line is. Jump start. You dive right back in." Momentum.

Robert Towne, *Chinatown,* always intro'd his anti-hero, page one. Describe any dynamic, unique physical or personality traits. Add some gag, like gum chewing. 'She always parks it behind her ear, grabbin' it later to rechew.' Whatever.

Waldo again. "Give your lead a personality flaw that often gets in their way. Have the hero overcome the flaw at story's end. A minor victory."

My personal addiction, bookending. I use a quirky sentence or phrase on page one that sort of sums up the spine of the story, then repeat it at the tale's end. Bookend closure.

Essential point from novel writer Philip Roth. "Your flawed hero must learn something crucial about life." Another minor victory.

Ever had a hot, fab idea, nothing to write it down on. By the time ya got to your laptop, idea's drifted into the ether, forever gone. Drats! Life saver! Use your iPhone to speak idea in *Notebooks app* after taping by using the microphone icon. Words appears on notebook screen. Then email note to yourself, open email, click *file* in top navigation bar, then *save as* RTF to desktop. On desktop *press/hold* control key and open RTF note on Microsoft Word, click *yes* on RTF drop down, idea opens. Save it as a Word doc, name it, save it. There ya go, ready to clean up. I've written entire stories on the go with this scheme. Try it. You'll feel like a pro by the second time you use it.

Times have changed since I've been in the biz. Now a *techmeister* world.

Tech has put filmmaking into your bedroom studio. Still, there are basics that will never change. Old cliché, fire in the belly, just as apt today as when I started my trek. You gotta relentlessly ram through every obstacle, take every "no" as a "yes," treat every failure as success or stay home, flipping burgers. Learn as you burn. Rejection, name of the game. Love it or leave it. Whatever rejects us makes us stronger. Grow a mylar titanium hide that nothing will ding. Move as a warrior through a realm that will test you to your limits. The experience will transform you. Crash and burn, not an option. Embrace the myth of the Phoenix, continually reborn from its ashes. Believe in your warrior self to sustain, prevail.

When that last page of your masterwork floats into the full box, run it by countless alpha readers. Once. Twice. Thrice. Keep the good feedback, trash the bad. If possible, find the funds to hire a pro editor to polish your gem. Money well spent.

Now time to let it fly. Today's production companies seldom accept screenplays that are not submitted by an agent. Getting on isn't easy. Google 'Talent Agencies'. Pick twenty. Send your screenplay, a covering letter, plus a slick three-page summary. Your elevator pitch that you'll scooby at your first meeting.

A new tactic, turn your screenplay into a novel, self-publish. Online startups to help you navigate that world are popping up. Production companies seem more impressed by a novel then a screenplay. They've seen thousands, but books have a stature that scripts do not. This is a unique way of getting a screenplay deal. The best part, the screenplay is already written. If you take this route, hire a professional literary editor to shine up your novel. Publish it on Amazon's Kindle Direct Publishing, merch it relentlessly, to online networks and production companies. Again, step one a book attention grabber. It's a double whammy. Screenplay, novel. Hit the industry with both under your arm.

One last over used buzz word, "Brand," a must. Your brand is you and your work. Build a website if ya ain't got one. Use social media to steer people to your website, you're your band prominent. Market the heck out of your band.

It takes superhuman strength to endure the dark forest of the film industry. Believe beyond doubt you can do it. Better yet, know that you can do it. Learn as you do it. You will succeed. Failure is not an option. Attack the film Gargantua, both coasts. Slay the beast. Personal must. Stay healthy. Apt cliché, your body is your temple. You will need it to dwell in as you pursue your never-ending hero's odyssey.

Feel free to track me down via my website, *Mick Benderoth.com*.

Now, back to where I started. Hang in. Keep truckin'. I'll keep a sharp eye out for your epic soon streaming the network multiverse. *Bonne chance.*

Mick Benderoth, New York, 2023

250

About The Author

Mick Benderoth is a New York filmmaker, TV commercial director, Hollywood screenwriter, and rock & roll musician. He spent twenty years in Hollywood as a screenwriter before returning to New York to start a television commercial production company. His wife Nancy produced while Mick directed. The company grew exponentially, becoming one of the most successful TV commercial boutiques in the city.

After ten years, they sold the company and moved to their house in East Hampton where Mick jumped into a new field, the theater. He wrote plays while Nancy returned to her first love, oil painting. Mick's play, *Brotherhood*, was performed in regional theaters.

He produced and edited the Warner Bros. documentary, *Malcolm X*, which was nominated for an Academy Award, later becoming Spike Lee's acclaimed dramatic film *Malcom X* starring Denzel Washington.

A veteran rock & roller from the 50's, Mick is still writing tunes and jamming with his grandson Griffin. His band Silverback's music is available for purchase on Amazon and iTunes.

His early short films *Abraxas*, and *A Beautiful Day for A Picnic*, won awards at The Atlanta, Maryland, and Philadelphia film festivals.

Mick now resides in Manhattan, writing and publishing fictional prose in all genres. His new books, *Macabres*, quirky tales of horror, and *Flix*, his story twists on autobiography, are available on Amazon. Some of Mick's stories have previously been published on genre web sites.

For more information, visit his website at MickBenderoth.com.

www.ingramcontent.com/pod-product-compliance
Lightning Source LLC
LaVergne TN
LVHW011322080426
835513LV00006B/158